German Army Handbook
1939-1945

FRONTISPIECE: The routine of war: A light AA gun mounted on a half-track carrier being used against ground targets in Russia, 1942. Division is **SS** Leibstandarte Adolf Hitler.   (STT 884)

German
Army
Handbook
1939-1945

W. J. K. Davies

LONDON

IAN ALLAN

First Published 1973

SBN 7110 0290 8

Published by Ian Allan Ltd, Shepperton, Surrey and printed in the United
Kingdom by Cox & Wyman Ltd, London, Fakenham and Reading.

Contents

List of Plates

List of Diagrams

List of Tables

Preface

Some explanation may be useful here as to the layout and terminology of the tables and diagrams. First, metric units have been used throughout since they are more accurate than conversions and since the onset of metrication will make them more useful. German terms – for instance in unit designations – have been used where confusion might arise and where they avoid clumsy rephrasing; as an example the army used three names for battalion-sized units: bataillon; sturmbann (SS); and abteilung, depending on what the unit was and in what area of the service it worked. In addition the diagrams showing composition of units follow the German pattern since this seems to me to be clearer than tabular form. The internal captions have been anglicised where necessary.

Acknowledgements

I would like to acknowledge the help of a number of people but in particular the staff of the Imperial War Museum library and photographic library who always provide unflagging assistance to researchers. Denis Bishop produced the splendid coloured plates.

Wheathampstead, 1972.

W. J. K. Davies

Introduction

This book is an attempt, at a moderate price, to fill a gap in military literature. When I started, some years ago, to investigate the armies of World War 2, I found little detailed information readily available; what there was, was often in the form of intelligence surveys which had the two disadvantages of describing an army only at a specific period and of containing inaccuracies inevitable when information was not freely available to their compilers. Since then an absolute flood of books has appeared but almost all deal in very great detail with one particular aspect of an army.

This, therefore, is intended simply as a basic reference manual and as a guide to readers of the many histories. It tries to answer the odd questions that arise when making first acquaintance with a subject . . . what was a Tellermine and what did it look like; how did a 'Mark IV' tank differ from a 'Mark III'; what was '*Keil und Kessel*' and why was it so called. It is not really for the specialist: he will not find super-detailed studies of a particular vehicle. Nor is it primarily for the modeller since the diagrams of equipment and weapons are really recognition sketches to cover those items not shown in photographs; though these are to the same general scale for comparison purposes. It will, I hope, however provide enough information for the average reader to build up a general picture, or for the war gamer to make a start; and it will give guidance on further study for anyone who wishes to pursue some particular specialisation.

I
Historical Background

It is probably safe to say that the German regular army was, in 1939, the most efficient national fighting force in the world. This was not necessarily because of its oft-quoted superiority of equipment, which was partly a propaganda myth that worked; the 'standard' and really efficient equipment was in general only in small scale use right up to the end of the 1940 French campaign and even later. It was due more to the tradition of militarism in the German nation, a tradition that ensured even in peace time an excellent and forward-looking General Staff and an army and population whose patriotism, and hence their military morale, could be easily stirred; and to the above-mentioned propaganda element which gave extra strength to the advanced tactics that were being adopted. The exaggerated accounts of the opening campaign against Poland in 1939 hid the fact that the successful Blitzkrieg (lightning war) had been achieved with quite ordinary equipment for the period, and thus helped to confuse and dishearten the opposition when the same tactics were used in France the following year. French equipment then, especially in armour, was in many ways superior to equivalent German machines but the army organisation was ineffective against the superb staff work and unexpected tactics of the Germans.

The basis of this military machine can be traced back to traditions of conscription and militarism, well before even the First World War, when the German General Staff never really thought of the army as having been defeated. This attitude, together with the resentment engendered by the Versailles treaty that among other things severely restricted weapons and armed forces, gave a boost to militarism that was showing results even before Hitler came to power in 1933. With hindsight it would seem that the Versailles restrictions on armament in particular did much to pressure Germany into developing technically advanced equipment and tactics so that, when the time came, an efficient army could be produced at short notice.

In consequence, through the late 1920s and early 1930s, in all arms basic equipment was being developed in civilian guises without the handicap of having to conserve existing material – the old story of the German worker who stole perambulator parts and found that on assembly they kept coming out as a machine gun, had more than a grain of truth in it. Certainly 'commercial' car and lorry chassis turned suspiciously easily into military cross-country vehicles, while more potent weapons were actually developed and tested fairly openly in neighbouring countries. Thus when Hitler came to power and declared the creation of a revived armed services (die *Wehrmacht,* comprising *das Heer* (Army); die *Luftwaffe* (Air Force); die *Kriegsmarine* (Navy)) the basic work had already been done in many cases. True, the development of battle tanks had been slowed, as had the development of artillery – they were big things to hide in the finished form – but other equipment was almost ready for production.

Unfortunately the General Staff and the propaganda branch let themselves be carried away by their ideals. In 1936, for example, the *Einheits,* or standard, vehicle programme provided for construction of a whole range of elaborate troop, supply and weapons carriers most of which had cross-country capability and all of which were very expensive. It became rapidly obvious that to provide even the limited striking forces required by the new tactics would take far too long and be far too costly. A rapid revaluation had to be undertaken and in 1938 Colonel von Schell pushed through a revised equipment programme that drastically simplified army procurement and introduced common elements in both civilian and army vehicles.

Organisation and planning, on the other hand, was not seriously inhibited by post-war restrictions and was pushed ahead urgently all through the inter-war period. Untouched by the 'allied' concept of apparently preparing for the next war on the lines of the last, the German General Staff seized on the ideas of the British Captain Liddel Hart who was advocating the development of armoured striking forces as the spearhead of an army. His concept was of the 'expanding torrent', the smashing hammerblow through an enemy front by masses of armour and mobile infantry which protected its flanks simply by its own speed and by the disorganisation it caused. The Germans developed this into the *Blitzkrieg* system which added to the tanks and infantry a force of ground attack aircraft to co-operate closely with the army and help to clear the way for the spearhead.

The thinking was sound; the snag was that, even with simplified equipment programmes, German industry could not produce nearly enough offensive equipment to meet the army's needs. The original plan was for 63 armoured (*Panzer*) Divisions; at the end of 1939 there were but ten and in 1945 there were only some 36, while it was impossible to keep even these fully equipped. Hence the Blitzkrieg concept virtually dictated the formation of the rest of the army. Apart from a limited number of motorised infantry divisions to back up the panzers, all infantry formations would have to rely mainly on horsedrawn transport, being carried and supplied by rail over long distances. It was considered that this was not of great importance since they were intended only as fairly static units, mopping up after the short sharp panzer war and garrisoning occupied districts. Time invalidated this theory but only because the Blitzkrieg, while winning major battles, did not in Russia provide the short sharp war it was intended to do.

Nonetheless, none of this was apparent in 1939. The political side is not relevant to this book except where it affected the army as a fighting machine but it had by then contributed in several ways to army tactical efficiency. One major one was in the annexation of Czechoslovakia which, from the military point of view, provided mobilisation practice – and an efficient battle-tank to stop the gap until home-developed machines came along! More than a quarter of the tanks used in the 1940 French campaign were of Czech design. It had also, however, already started to reduce the independent decision-making power of the General Staff, a tendency that was eventually to subordinate military policy directly to the control of Hitler, and eventually to embarrass the army in many ways.

In the field, initially, the Blitzkrieg worked. With crushing air superiority and the unexpected tactics of the lightning war, first the Poles in Autumn 1939 and then the French and British eight months later were caught unprepared and decisively defeated on land. The German army found itself master of western Europe with a reputation for high fighting power and advanced equipment. The paucity of such equipment was not noticed and the success in some part seems to have hidden its lack even from the German political leaders.

During the ensuing year, much improved equipment, both light and heavy, was in fact coming into service. The main battle tanks Types III and IV, new infantry weapons, and tactics based upon the lessons learnt were ready for the major turning point of the war – the opening of the Russian front in June 1941. Although it exposed Germany to that constant General Staff nightmare, a war on two major fronts, at first this appeared a feasible operation. The panzer tactics and the sweeping outflanking movements worked; the opposition was driven back in great leaps and bounds. But it also very soon revealed the two basic weaknesses that defeated the German army.

Firstly, it became quickly evident that production capacity was not sufficient to equip properly the rapid expansion made necessary by the vast distances of Russia; a situation made worse by operations in the Balkans and in Africa which drained off further resources. The non-mobile infantry Divisions in

1. The army on parade in peacetime: Pzkw I tanks (Ausführung B) with, in the background, 4-wheeled touring-car pattern personnel carriers (Kübelwagen). (MH 8876)

particular proved a considerable handicap and the Russian winter of 1941–2 showed up a new weak link – unpreparedness to face extremely low temperatures. The wastage in vehicles, equipment and men was enormous and continual. The Blitzkrieg for the first time failed and in doing so sealed the final military defeat.

Secondly the strictly military control of operations was over. Even during the summer of 1941, central OKH control had grown so weak that individual army group commanders were interfering in the strategic planning by initiating operations on their own; OKH was finally emasculated when on December 19, 1941, Hitler took over direct command of the army and increasingly interfered in its activities. While the offensives were taking place this was not quite so serious but once, from late 1942 on, the army was forced on to the defensive on all fronts, its effects both on efficiency and morale became extremely serious. Hitler developed an obsession about not giving up ground, which lost vast quantities of men and material that the army could not spare; Germany had only a very limited potential in a long war and such epic disasters as Stalingrad and Tunis where whole armies of 100,000 men and more were lost complete with their equipment were largely irremediable so far as army strength was concerned. In addition his reaction to the 'independence' of the Russian front generals was to tie their hands by far too detailed orders which often could not take into account the actual circumstances in the field.

Here the political side of the war machine was a crippling handicap to the better field commanders, as it was in the rise of the 'private armies' formed by various factions within the Nazi regime. The most well-known of these was the *Waffen SS (Schutzstaffel)*, the armed branch of the Nazi Party's own force. From 1943 on, the best equipment, the best fighting men, the most regular supplies were directed into this army which totalled over 38 Divisions by the war's end. At its best it was an effective fighting force second to none but for the army command it had serious disadvantages.

First and foremost its field commanders always had a direct line of communication to Nazi headquarters and hence to OKW – the supreme command of the Wehrmacht; there was always a struggle for control in the field so that army commanders could never entirely assimilate SS units within their commands. Secondly its loyalty eventually was to its creator Heinrich Himmler and to Hitler, not to the army General Staff; thirdly, in its creator's quest for power, it soon included a number of almost completely useless Divisions sometimes known as the 'joke SS' or 'Byzantine SS' composed almost entirely of foreign nationals and criminals some of whom fought well but many of whom could be guaranteed to desert at the first opportunity; yet they still had to be employed in war and they still consumed valuable equipment.

On a lesser scale the same can be said for the field Divisions hastily formed during 1943–5 from redundant Luftwaffe and Kriegsmarine personnel. They were not trained to the standard of regular divisions, their equipment was not so good, and their former masters were always trying to keep some measure of control. Even the *Volksturm*, the last-ditch home guard that was blown up out of all proportion for political reasons by Martin Bormann – who wanted his own army – diverted some effort and equipment. As several commentators have said, it was a wonder that the poor regular army ever got any replacements at all!

On the credit side, however, political pressure had some rationalising effect on development and production. From 1942 on, new and for its period very advanced, equipment began to reach the field army, though never in sufficient quantity. Despite their teething troubles, the new tanks, guns, infantry carriers and light infantry weapons were superior in design to equivalent allied equipment and it was only this superiority of design, coupled to the still efficient military machine and the resilience of the average German soldier, that enabled the army to fight on for so long. For, from the time of the successful allied invasion of Normandy in June 1944, the original defects of the Army ensured its eventual destruction.

Firstly the basic lack of resources was emphasised by an ever increasing allied superiority in the air and an apparently inexhaustible allied source of equipment and manpower. If the Germans lost a thousand men or fifty tanks – or, more importantly, a fuel or ammunition dump – it was very difficult to replace them, especially as four fronts were calling for help. If the allies lost 100 tanks another 100 appeared as if by magic. Then, too, allied air superiority invalidated the German strategic defence pattern that had been forced on them by the split between mobile and largely immobile Divisions. On the western front, with rail traffic disrupted by air strikes, they could no longer easily move the horse-drawn infantry Divisions and had to rely on a crust defence backed by barely adequate mobile reserves. Yet allied air power also seriously hampered the mobility of these reserves. Petrol stores dropped rapidly and even heavy armour could not move safely in daylight. Thus even the panzer and motorised units, bled of much equipment for the Russian front, were drawn into the crust defence. It was a very hard crust to crack as the allies found at Caen and at Monte Cassino, but once it broke there was little to hold advancing troops and, more important, much equipment had to be abandoned through lack of transport. Matters were not made easier for the tactical commanders by Hitler's continued demands not to give ground, since it was then largely impossible to build up reserve lines or to conduct a proper strategic withdrawal.

On the Russian front, air superiority was never such a problem but the extremes of climate and the vast distances handicapped the German army in much the same way. There was never enough mobile transport or battle equipment and what there was wore out quickly. In the circumstances the German withdrawal was a good piece of tactical fighting since, until the Russians used Blitzkrieg tactics themselves in overwhelming strength in 1945, some sort of a front line was always maintained.

Perhaps the most amazing thing about the German army in fact is that, despite political interference, its losses and the impossibility of ever meeting its needs, it remained a cohesive organisation up to the end of the war. This was partly helped by the increasingly strict combing out of civilian workers to supply manpower needs and by the staggering capacity of German industry to maintain high production totals even under the allied bombing. Nonetheless it was a considerable feat to be able to raise a mobile counter attack force of the size and quality that tried to burst through the Ardennes in December 1944.

That the gamble failed through, almost inevitably, the German weaknesses of political interference, lack of fuel and the superior capacity of the allied forces especially in the air, does not conceal the basic feat.

In summary, the German army in the 1939–45 war suffered from the start by inadequate supplies of men and material. This would not have been vital had the Blitzkrieg philosophy always won campaigns instead of only major battles, but the Russian Blitzkrieg failed. From that time on the army was committed to a long drawn-out struggle on several fronts with inadequate mobility to maintain its front lines. The manpower and equipment situation was gravely worsened by political interference which threw away whole armies for militarily unsound reasons and this problem was compounded when the additional front was opened by the allied invasion of Europe. Lack of mobility in Russia and allied air superiority in France, together with political pressures, forced the adoption of a 'crust' defence. This in turn caused further heavy losses when the crust was broken. What enabled the army to fight so long so effectively under these circumstances was the adaptability of its organisation both for fighting and supply, the technical superiority of much of its equipment and a basic capacity to improvise. The Germans, through sheer necessity, were the first modern army to carry out the now fashionable doctrine of minimum manpower, maximum firepower. The average Division at full establishment in 1939 was 15–17,000 men. By 1945 manpower strength of a Division was down to 11–13,000 at full establishment but its total firepower, particularly in infantry weapons, had actually increased.

2. On parade in War: German infantry goose-stepping through a small French town on the Aisne in 1940. Note the early pattern tunics, Gewehr 98 rifles and the bicycle squad. (MH 9205)

2

Organisation and Administration of the German Army to Divisional Level

Basic Structure

The organisation of the regular army throughout the war was based on its peace-time structure, although some modifications took place from about 1942 on.

The original concept of the Army (*Das Heer*, as opposed to *Die Wehrmacht* which theoretically included all armed forces) was based on *Wehrkreise* or home-base areas of which there were eighteen in 1939, divided between six Army Groups; two were in Austria and of recent origin. (Fig 1.) Each Wehrkreis was 'home' to a number of divisions and, more important, to their component Regiments which each had a regimental base. At the commencement of full mobilisation in 1939 there were 51 divisions and two Brigades, each numbered in their own series and split up as follows:

39   Infantry Divisions (1–36; 44–46) of which Nos 2, 13, 20 and 29 were fully motorised and designated as such.
3   Mountain Divisions (1–3)
4   Light Divisions (1–4) – highly mobile mounted infantry formations
5   Panzer (armoured) Divisions (1–5)
1   Panzer Brigade (4 Pz Bde, converted to 10 Pz Div before the outbreak of war)
1   Cavalry Brigade (1 Kav. Bde) – partly mechanised.

The war mobilisation plan was based on the '*Ersatz*' system (NB that in German the word *ersatz* does not have the connotation 'shoddy' that English propaganda gave it; it simply means 'substitute' or 'replacement'). In this plan, each peace-time unit had two parts: the active unit already up to war strength, and a permanent 'replacement' cadre at its base. This could at short notice call up reservists, organise recruiting, carry out training and dispatch of replacement drafts and organise the reception and processing of wounded or convalescent personnel. In the Divisions, it was a separate headquarters staff known as a *Division Nummer* (Div Nr) which was purely an administrative organisation, although listed as a Division in the Order of Battle. For smaller units the cadre was in the nature of a Base HQ controlled by the appropriate Div Nr, which could raise extra battalions of the regiment or *Abteilung* – generally defined as an organic formation of battalion size.

The scheme was that, if war appeared imminent, second battalions could be raised and equipped from active reservists without showing much external sign of mobilisation, and additional reserve battalions could be provided fairly quickly thereafter, with appropriate divisional HQs. In practice, the system was extremely flexible and on the outbreak of war produced four 'waves' of infantry

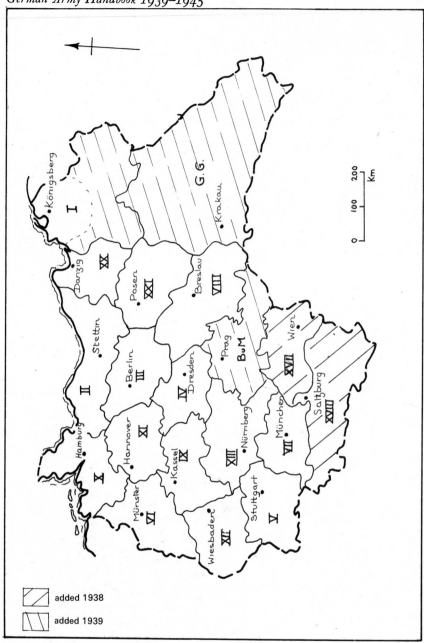

FIG 1   WEHRKREISE in 1940

Divisions, successively the active units, fresh reservists, *Landwehr* or territorials, and short-trained men of the 1901–13 classes. On the Panzer side, the original five divisions were quickly doubled in number mainly by converting the existing Light Divisions.

This system remained almost unaltered until 1942 although, after the first Russian campaign, a number of field replacement units were situated near the appropriate theatre of war instead of in their home *Wehrkreise*; in addition entirely new units were formed when and where required rather than with territorial associations. By late 1942, the Army had become so large and complicated that the Ersatz duties were split. The old Div Nr HQs became simply mobilisation organisations while new training units (*Ausbildungseinheiten*) were organised as Regimenter and Abteilungen. In 1943 some of these latter units on the Russian front were even organised as Divisions, fully armed and equipped to carry out local garrison and anti-partisan duties, being known first as *Feldersatzdivisionen* and then as *Feldausbildungsdivisionen*. The responsibility for them was then transferred from the Ersatz organisation to the field, or fighting, army.

THE FIELD ARMY (Feldheer)

ARMY HIGH COMMAND: All German armed forces were controlled by the *Führerhauptquartier* (Führer's HQ) through the *Oberkommando der Wehrmacht* (OKW), of which Hitler, as Head of State, was titular supreme commander. Under this came the theoretically autonomous service headquarters of which the army one was OKH (*Oberkommando des Heeres*). In December 1941, Hitler for various reasons also assumed direct command of the army, leaving the commander in chief as increasingly little more than a cipher. The notional organisation, however, remained unaltered. OKH had twelve departments, each having overall responsibility for one aspect of the Army. The arrangement was very similar to that of other armies with the exception of the Army Administration Office (*Heeresverwaltungsamt*) which was broadly responsible for the procurement of rations, billets, pay and clothing – but not for munitions supply. This was staffed by its own corps of technical and administrative specialists whose careers were entirely separated from the normal army personnel channels and were controlled by their own corps. These men, termed *Wehrmachtbeamten* (normally translated 'officials' by allied Intelligence) operated as a unified corps throughout the army, being attached to field units right down to company level. They wore uniform, were regarded as combatants – most front line Beamten held officer rank – and received a basic infantry training. After May 1944, they lost some of their independence, promotion and transfers then becoming a responsibility of the Army Personnel Department.

ARMY COMMAND ORGANISATION TO DIVISIONAL LEVEL: The organisation of the field army is shown in Fig. 2. It should be noted that the number of Army Groups expanded as the war went on; that the number of Armies in a Group, Corps in an Army and Divisions in a Corps could vary widely depending on the campaign situation; that the system was flexible and it was possible to reform and change the number and type of fighting formations at all levels from Army downward. Three other points are worth noting:

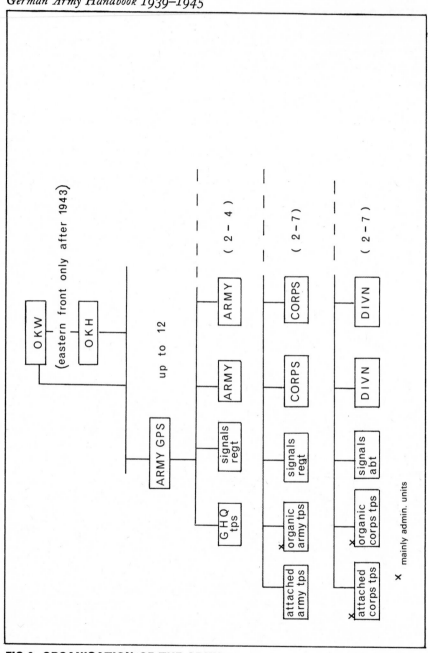

FIG 2 ORGANISATION OF THE ARMY

(i) Armies and Corps were, at least theoretically, of one type only (eg Panzer Army). There were four basic patterns of army – Panzer, Infantry, Mountain and Parachute – and six types of Corps: Panzer, Infantry, Mountain, Parachute, Corps Command (HQ and organic troops only), and Reserve. In practice any of these could contain elements of another if the situation warranted it, or if it suddenly had to take over reserves or an additional section of front line.

(ii) 'Organic' troops at Army and Corps level were largely the services and administrative units required by any major formation in an organisation with a clear chain of command (eg field post offices, police, engineers). For this purpose Corps were regarded as fighting control headquarters and had fewer organic units, especially as regards supply.

(iii) 'Attached' troops at Army and Corps level were fighting and specialist units. OKH allocated such units semi-permanently to Army Groups who exercised overall planning control of them. (These are called GHQ troops by allied Intelligence, and for convenience, this term will be used henceforward). Armies were then allocated a proportion of these units, depending on their campaign requirements, and they in turn doled them out to Corps on a temporary basis. The units (see p. 52) included heavy armour, artillery and engineer brigades or battalions, together with specialist units such as decontamination companies and chemical warfare units.

The main fighting units were, as in all contemporary armies, the Divisions, whose composition will be described in detail in Chapter 3. Briefly, in 1939, they consisted of the troops listed on p. 19 together with *'Grenzwach'* or

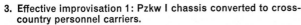

3. Effective improvisation 1: Pzkw I chassis converted to cross-country personnel carriers.

frontier troops. As the war progressed and it became necessary to administer and garrison occupied territories, further types such as the *Sicherungsdivision* (security) and the coast defence division were formed, and pressures on manpower led also to the formation of some improvised units such as the '*sturm*' or assault division which had fewer troops but an increase in automatic firepower, and the *Volksgrenadier* divisions composed mainly of men combed out from civilian employment and equipped on a lower scale than regular formations. It may be noted that the use of such imposing titles became more frequent especially for low grade formations as the war progressed and the troops' morale needed boosting. For example all infantry units were theoretically termed 'grenadier' units after 1943, leading to some confusion with the true *panzer grenadiere* or armoured infantry; and traditional titles were often revived for new formations or those given a particularly onerous role. Thus some of the new infantry units formed from 1941 on for Balkans service were termed *Jaeger* divisions (usually translated 'light divisions') to symbolise a link with the former light infantry units of the old Prussian empire; and the recce or mobile reserve battalions of some infantry divisions were known as 'Fusilier' units commemorating the former Germanic rifle skirmishers.

These comments apply only to the regular army; the so-called 'private armies', notably the SS and the Luftwaffe ground troops, were in many ways a law unto themselves and were only tactically under army control. Thus, although in theory the chain of command was clear, as the war progressed it was

4. Improvisation 2: An early self-propelled weapon comprising a heavy infantry gun sIG33 mounted complete on an obsolete tank chassis leads panzer troops through a French village. Of interest are the style of cross and the Divisional sign above a white G (for Guderian). (MH 9419)

not only interfered with by other organisations, but Hitler himself short-circuited it more and more frequently, often giving direct orders to front-line commanders over the heads of their superiors. Indeed, after 1943, OKH controlled the Eastern fronts only, the others being directly under OKW.

ADMINISTRATION AND SUPPLY ORGANISATION TO DIVISIONAL LEVEL: The organisation of German army supply and administration services was generally conceded to be very efficient; even up to the final months of the war, allied Intelligence reports were commenting in some surprise on how well a beaten army could yet hold together, and they were certainly efficient enough to organise support for the Ardennes offensive of December 1944 at a time when the allies reckoned that the whole army organisation should have been in chaos.

The secret lay in simple administration with few and clearly defined spheres of responsibility, a basic structure which could be rapidly expanded or contracted as the military situation dictated, and an ability to utilise local resources to the maximum. In particular the two functions of transport and handling were clearly separated. Fig. 3 shows the basic system of pushing forward supplies which, with minor variations, was applicable to all items.

TRANSPORT: Down to Divisional level, this was the responsibility of the Senior Supply Officer at Army, who had at his disposal a number of standardised units known as *Kolonne* or Columns. The six major types and capacities were:

(i) *Fahrkolonne:* Horse-drawn unit with a capacity of 30 tonnes.
(ii) *Leichte Fahrkolonne:* As above but of 17 tonnes capacity.
(iii) *Leichte Kraftwagen Kolonne:* A motorised column of 30 tonnes capacity.
(iv) *Schweres Kraftwagen Kolonne:* As above but of 60 tonnes.
(v) *Leichte Kraftwagen Kolonne für Betriebstoff:* MT fuel column with a capacity of 5,500 gallons.
(vi) *Schweres Kraftwagen Kolonne:* As above but carrying 11,000 gallons.

All except (iv) were commonly found also as parts of the organic units within divisions and as components of the Divisional services which had a normal allocation of eight or nine columns of various types, the composition depending on the Division. It should be noted that Corps, as such, played a very small part in supply although later in the war it often *controlled* the forward supply dumps.

Transport within Divisional units was divided into unit supply (baggage, rations, etc) which was provided by the light columns, and unit battle transport (*Gefechtstross*) which was issued down to company level and carried the ready-use supplies and equipment. It was quite common, especially when the organisation was streamlined towards the end of the war, for unit supply transport to be taken under Regimental or even Divisional control where this was deemed necessary.

HANDLING: Formations down to Regiment level had special units known as supply companies (*Nachschubkompanien*) or, at Army, battalions (*Nachschubabteilungen*). These provided the labour for actually unloading and reloading consumable supplies and were controlled by special administration platoons; the only major exception was in the case of motor fuel where handling was

5. Panzer troops in action: Panzer grenadiers dismount from their armoured transport. The vehicles are Sd Kfz 251s, the rear one being a platoon commander's vehicle with a 3·7cm anti-tank gun. (MH 200)

undertaken largely by trained men of the transport columns. It was a basic rule that supplies were taken as far forward as possible without transhipment.

REPAIR AND REPLACEMENT OF EQUIPMENT: All major units had first line repair and maintenance sub-units to cope with running repairs, and Divisions had workshop companies for harder tasks. If a repair job was too big for these it was passed back direct to Army which maintained fully equipped field workshops capable of complete rebuilds and also had 'parks' – units which acted as reception and issue organisations for weapons and equipment. Army in turn might return vehicles and weapons to the OKH pool for onward transmission to the manufacturers and would indent on GHQ or Army Group for new stores.

OTHER SUPPLIES: It is not possible here to detail all the supply organisations (eg medical or veterinary). Suffice to say that these were generally on the same principles: to and from unit – division – direct to army, and thence to and from home area (Wehrkreis) and that, with so many horse-drawn divisions the veterinary services in particular were comprehensive. All were characterised by the same simplicity and flexibility of organisation, enabling intermediate stages of supply to be bypassed easily if the tactical situation demanded.

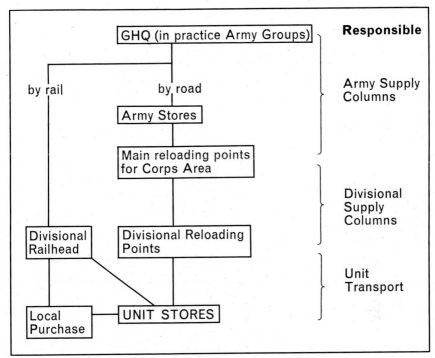

FIG 3 PATTERN OF SUPPLY IN THE FIELD

6. On the Russian front, panzer grenadiers advance. Vehicles are standard Sd Kfz 251s, but fitted with side racks to take Werferrahmen (p. 113). The large numbers in white appear to indicate individual vehicles within the unit. (MH 210)

3
Divisions and Other Major Fighting Units

The Division was, in all armies of the Second World War, the biggest organic or cohesive unit with a balanced allocation of all arms and capable of acting as an independent whole. Corps troops were normally specialised units used only to add weight to a particular arm for a specific operation; Army troops, even more, were heavy units not very happy on their own. A division could at least theoretically support itself.

It included at least some form of scouting or reconnaissance unit, special signals and engineer units, the latter often equipped for light bridging operations, an infantry component of at least four and often up to nine battalions, an artillery regiment, and various supply, support and disciplinary services to keep it running in the field. Additionally it might include one or more armoured units to provide strength in attack if that was its mission in life.

At this point, a note on German unit nomenclature may be appropriate since it differed from, and in some cases clashed with, our own. The biggest organic (ie self-sufficient) unit in a division was the *Regiment* (hard 'g'), roughly the equivalent of a British Brigade, which was divided into *Abteilungen*. These were equivalent to a British infantry battalion, tank regiment or artillery regiment – though somewhat smaller than the latter. Each Abteilung had several '*Kompanien*' or artillery '*batterie*' (the latter equalling a British 'troop' and sometimes described as such in translations). The Companies were divided into '*Züge*' (s. zug), the rough equivalent of a British platoon. Organic units of battalion size or above (eg the recce unit) were normally classed as Abteilungen and the term *Brigade* was reserved for groups of two or more *Regimenten* or for organic combined units of similar size (eg *Panzer Brigade*). The Germans did also use the obsolete term '*Bataillon*' in its normal sense as indicating a battalion, particularly in engineer units and infantry division recce units after 1944.

Types of Division

In the German army the major fighting Divisions were of sharply contrasted types owing to the Blitzkrieg philosophy. This called for a limited number of very well equipped, highly mobile 'hitting divisions' backed by less strong but fully mechanised infantry formations to provide swift follow-up in the attack. The major snag was that, given the known capacity of the German production industry, this meant that concentration on the elite divisions left very little spare capacity to supply transport and mobile weapons for the remainder. This the OKH did not consider so important; the line infantry were expected only to consolidate gains and occupy enemy territory, or to hold fairly static portions of front line. Thus they were intended to be transported largely by rail, an excellent military railways department being a useful legacy of the previous war. For tactical purposes and short range supply from railhead they could be equipped mainly with horse-drawn transport which theoretically could be supplemented locally with material requisitioned in occupied territory. Their weapons, too, could be more defensive in pattern than those of the *Panzer*, or armoured Divisions and did not require such expensive and sophisticated mobile carriages.

There has been a strong tendency to mock at the German army because of the archaic nature of this equipment scale but the criticism is not entirely fair. Given that the original Blitzkrieg premise was sound, the idea of a railway-transported unit using modern horse-drawn transport was perfectly viable, and the intended equipment – light, steel-bodied and pneumatic tyred – was probably as efficient as horse-drawn vehicles could be. What went wrong was, in the incredible wastages following the opening up of the Russian front, and again in Normandy, line infantry Divisions had to be used in a more mobile situation than first envisaged, while once air superiority was lost rail transport became very vulnerable. The subsequent wastage of equipment also meant that much archaic World War I pattern transport had to be pressed into use, further aggravating a deteriorating situation.

As with other armies there were also other, more specialised, Divisions such as mountain troops, parachute units and, later on, various low-grade formations such as the Luftwaffe (Air Force) field Divisions, fortress troops and the *Volksgrenadier* divisions – usually made up either of virtually untrained troops or of the very scrapings from the manpower barrel: convalescents who should not have returned to military service, those with similar ailments often grouped for ease of medical attention, young boys of 15 or so, and old men nearing retiring age. All, however, had one thing in common with the 'regular' fighting Divisions: they were built on what one might call the plug-in unit principle.

This philosophy required a balanced allocation of arms right through the Division down to platoon or even section level, so that any of its combatant units could operate as a self-contained force on its own level and could be quickly combined with other scratch units without upsetting the balance of arms. Thus the Division as a unit backed its infantry with anti-tank gun and artillery Abteilungen; an infantry Regiment had two or three Abteilungen with, ideally, an anti-tank company and a close-support gun company; an Abteilung within the regiment had three rifle companies and a heavy company with medium and heavy mortars and heavy machine guns; the rifle company had three rifle platoons and a heavy platoon with mortars and machine guns; a platoon had its own light anti-tank weapon and a 5cm – later an 8cm – mortar. In practice things did not always work out quite so neatly of course but the principle was there and it greatly facilitated the quick extemporisation of 'battlegroups' (*Kampfgruppen*) from one or more units to meet some local emergency, a facility the Germans exploited to the full. It no doubt contributed also to the fact that ordinary German soldiers appeared willing and able to fight under the direction of any officer rather than clinging to the sort of loyalty a British soldier showed to 'his' unit – and the subsequent frequent anxiety and loss of efficiency if removed from it at short notice. The principle also had a major disadvantage in that heavy weapons were dispersed throughout the Division. Hence though each unit always had some localised support it was almost impossible for, say, all the Divisional artillery to be easily concentrated in the same devastating manner that a British artillery commander could mass his 25-pounder regiments.

Another general feature of the German Divisional organisation was that not only the nominal rifle regiments were effective combatant infantry. The recce Abteilung, unlike the British and American armoured car units, included a strong infantry component mounted, in the case of mobile Divisions, on fast cars, motorcycles or armoured troop carriers, and in infantry Divisions provided at least with bicycles or horses! Thus they could form a mobile reserve and were backed up by the engineers. These were also fully combatant and organised as a strong infantry battalion with its full complement of heavy weapons, including flamethrowers. Indeed they were often the toughest troops in the Division and specialised in assault work.

The effectiveness of all these elements, as of the purely Divisional units such as the anti-tank Abteilung and, where appropriate, the tank regiment, depended of course on what equipment was available and what the Division was expected to do. There was not, despite all the beautifully drawn Intelligence diagrams, a standard establishment for any type of unit above battalion level, after the first year or so of the war. Constant wastage and the continual acquisition and conversion of captured equipment meant that when a Division was formed or refitted it often received units varying quite widely in strength and type of

7. The desert, 1: A typical view of battle aftermath; an 8t standard
half track (Sd Kfz 7) and 8·8cm flak gun in typical desert scenery.
(MH 181)

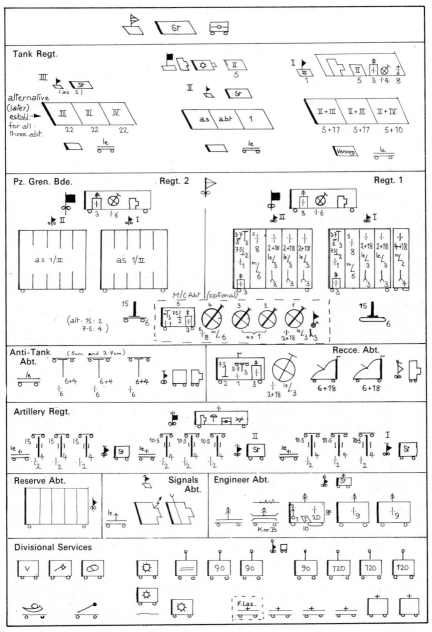

FIG 4 PANZER DIVISION 1941–2

equipment from the notional 'standard'. This applied particularly in later war years when few even of the mobile Divisions were up to full strength and, in particular, used large numbers of 'ersatz' vehicles in place of their official complement. For example, 24 Panzer Division at a crucial stage of the Russian campaign was supposed to have a Panther and a Type IV tank battalion. Its Panther battalion was non-existent – there were never enough to go round – and its Type IV unit was equipped largely with long-barrelled assault guns in default of its proper tanks.

In practice it would appear that there were three varieties of establishment at Divisional level. First came the basic 'type establishment', or *Grund Glieder-ung*, issued by the OKH as a standard pattern for a particular type (eg *Infantry Division Typ 1944*), and couched in such general terms that it often specified only calibres of weapons or even just whether they were 'light' (le) or 'heavy' (s); most of the order of battle charts in this chapter are taken from the appro-priate Grund Gliederung. Within each 'type', however, Divisions were raised often in batches or waves *(Wellen)* and the decreed establishment for each Welle might well differ from the Grund Gliederung then in force, depending on the current supply of manpower and material. This, the *Soll Gliederung* or intended establishment, showed for a particular Division or group of Divisions what it was thought could be achieved in practice; typical changes would be different anti-tank gun calibres (eg 4·7cm instead of 5cm). What was achieved, was shown by the *'Ise Gliederung'* or actual establishment that indicated the Divi-sion's strength at a particular point in its history and often radically different from what was hoped for! The position is slightly complicated by the fact that official establishments normally allocated each Division a field replacement unit *(Feldersatzabteilung)* which was supposed to keep in reserve the equivalent of a complete infantry battalion with a selection of spare light and heavy weapons. In the field this was likely to disappear almost as soon as the Division entered combat and to become merely an administrative unit for receiving and processing replacements. It therefore rarely appears in allied Intelligence reports.

Thus organisations changed at various periods, usually as there was need to conserve resources, and the notes that follow are intended to reflect this where possible. The only ones not noted are the so-called *1945-Typ* establishments. The reason is that, while such Establishments were issued from March 1945 on for both Infantry and Panzer Divisions, the battle situation was so fluid that they were hardly used since units could not be released; only three or four infantry Divisions and possibly one Panzer formation were in process of refitting to the standards at the final collapse. In general they envisaged drastic reductions in manpower and heavy equipment, the *Panzer Division Typ 1945* indeed being renamed *Panzer Division Kampfgruppe Typ 1945*, almost as soon as it was issued; it envisaged a 1944-pattern Panzer brigade (p. 49) backed by some additional infantry in weak regiment strength, some artillery and reduced Divisional Services.

PANZER (ARMOURED) DIVISION

(*Panzer* equals armour and, hence, 'Tank' – a more logical derivation than our own word. The term is an abbreviation from *Panzerkampfwagen* (armoured

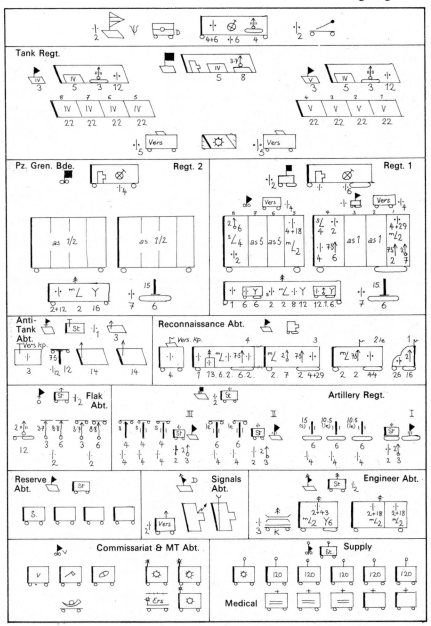

FIG 5 PANZER DIVISION Typ 1944

battle vehicle) and the correct past tense is 'gepanzerte' (gp) used in describing various units within the Division.)

The Panzer Division was the hitting power of the German army. Pre-war there were only five but they were increased to ten by 1940 and before the war's end there were 27 army Divisions, 1 Luftwaffe one, and 7 SS ones. The army Divisions initially comprised two full tank regiments totalling some 400 tanks, with a small infantry component and supporting services. These tanks, however, were mainly the light Pzkw I and II, virtually armoured machine gun or light cannon carriers, with an admixture of Czech machines and a few heavier vehicles. The French campaign in 1940, when the Panzers far outran their following infantry divisions, showed the manifold dangers of such an organisation and late in 1940 they were reorganised on a much better balanced basis with one tank regiment, two motorised infantry regiments and stronger supporting units. In particular self-propelled anti-tank guns and artillery were introduced progressively to increase the offensive power and in the case of SS Divisions especially the infantry component was often further strengthened. The Panzer Divisions always got the pick of the equipment but in 1944–5 particularly, even this was not enough and the SS Divisions were the only ones to be maintained at anywhere near full strength with standard vehicles. Under Divisional HQ with its support company (communications, local defence, survey, etc) were:

ARMOURED RECONNAISSANCE UNIT (*Panzeraufklärungsabteilung*): This was a very effective fighting unit with heavy and light armoured cars, two or three

8. Desert 2: a nose-to-tail transport column of 21 Panzer Division with Einheits-programme personnel carriers of the 8th infantry company; in front are light standard cars. (HU 5615)

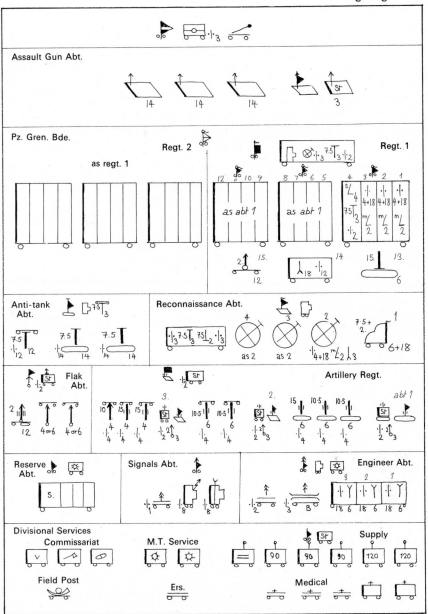

FIG 6 PANZER GRENADIER DIVISION

infantry companies and a heavy company that included self-propelled (SP) anti-tank and close support guns and an engineer platoon. The light armoured car company was often mounted in modified half-tracks and might in practice be the third infantry company, while the infantry could be in half-tracks or, especially on the Russian front, in Volkswagens or motorcycles. There were many permutations on this arrangement!

TANK REGIMENT (*Panzer Regiment*): In the 1941–2 organisation this consisted of three battalions, each of two companies of Type III battle tanks and a company of short-gunned Type IVs for close support work. It also had a reconnaissance troop of Type IIs attached to Battalion HQ. Later the allocation was changed to two battalions of four companies, one of 96 Type IV and one of 96 Panthers, often with a ninth company of Tiger tanks or assault guns; this latter addition was most frequently found in Russia and from 1944 on was not common, the heavy tanks being organised in separate units. In practice, while great efforts were made to keep the Type IV battalions up to strength there were never enough Panthers to go round and various captured vehicles and other ersatz machines were at times substituted – for example 21 Panzer, at the Normandy invasion had one battalion equipped with French vehicles of rather dubious value. The recce troop disappeared, its place being taken by an HQ allocation of five tanks of the same type as equipped the tank companies, while up to ten Pz II or III flamethrowing tanks could be attached to the Regiment. Various SP anti-tank and AA guns were also included together with maintenance and repair units.

PANZER GRENADIER BRIGADE: This consisted of two mechanised and well-equipped infantry regiments normally of two abteilungen each – although certain SS Divisions had three-abteilung regiments and a few even had three regiments. As soon as possible after 1940–41, one of the four abteilungen was mounted in half-tracked armoured personnel carriers and dubbed armoured (gepanzerte) its parent regiment also being referred to as armoured; this abteilung had a big allocation of heavy mobile weapons including 2cm AA/AT guns and no less than twelve 7·5cm SP close-support guns. Each regiment also had engineer, AA, and SP infantry gun companies, light anti-tank equipment being integrated in the infantry Abteilungen, though rarely shown on standard establishment charts.

ANTI-TANK BATTALION (*Panzerjaegerabteilung*): This developed rapidly during the war as anti-tank weapons themselves developed. It was always an integral part of the attacking power of the Division, its mission in attack being to safeguard the tank regiment's flanks. For this reason, during the period 1941–4 it was, in theory at least, equipped entirely with self-propelled guns, fourteen in each of three companies. Initially they were the light 4·7cm and 5cm guns mounted on obsolete tank chassis and supplemented by ex-Russian 7·62cm and German 7·5cm guns similarly mounted; later a standardised issue of proper 7·5cm anti-tank guns was provided, usually long-barrelled assault guns or the specialised Type III/IV *Jagdpanzer* (hunter tanks). Some divisions also had an allocation of SP or towed 8·8cm guns, especially on the Russian front, although these were more frequently found under Corps control. In the later stages of the war a revised allocation took account of the defensive nature

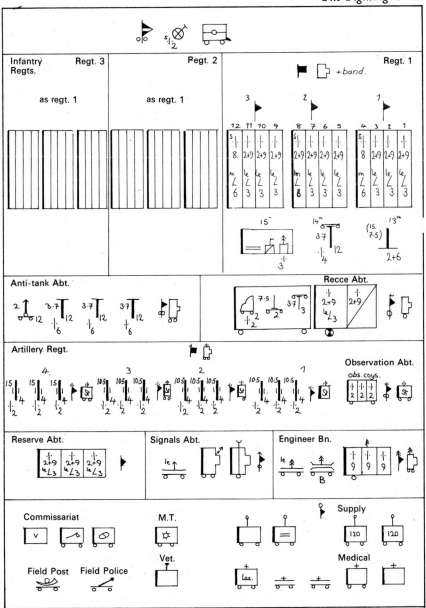

FIG 7 INFANTRY DIVISION 1939

of the fighting and the shortage of SP equipment. Divisions on the western front in particular then had two companies of SP guns and one company of towed 7·5s.

ANTI AIRCRAFT BATTALION (*Flak Abteilung*): The AA unit was controlled by the army and for most of the war comprised two heavy batteries of four or six 8·8cm dual purpose towed guns each, and one light battery of 2cm guns, twelve in all. It was sometimes incorporated in the artillery Regiment, and could include a few 3·7cm guns.

ARTILLERY REGIMENT: This normally comprised three abteilungen, one being a strong mixed SP unit of Wespe and Hummel, 18 in all (see p. 108). The second comprised three batteries of four towed 10·5cm gun-howitzers each and the third was a similar unit of 15cm towed gun-howitzers. This latter often had one battery replaced by four 10cm guns but these could also be found as an extra independent battery together with up to six 15cm rocket projectors. SS Divisions sometimes had a complete independent abteilung of these heavy projectors and an additional assault gun abteilung as well.

9. Severe conditions in the mountains: mountain troops with one of the few available views of a Geb.36 7·5cm light gun. (STT 3150)

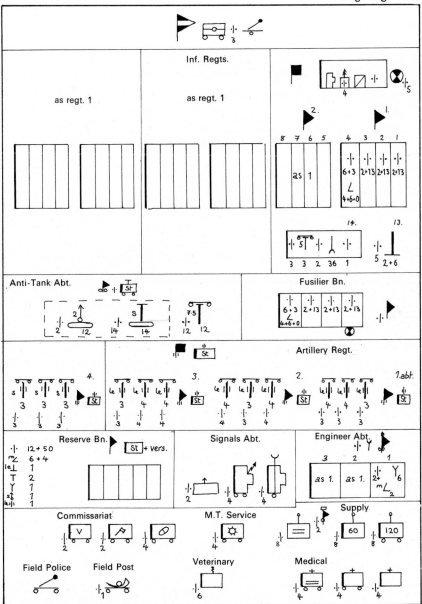

FIG 8   INFANTRY DIVISION 1944

ENGINEERS (*Pioniere*) AND SIGNALS (*Nachrichten*): These were both organic abteilungen. The armoured signals battalion was not a fighting unit but the armoured engineer Abteilung most certainly was. It consisted of two or three strong infantry companies, one mounted in armoured troop carriers the others motorised; one or two bridging columns, often with armoured vehicles; and a light engineer column.

DIVISIONAL SERVICES: These were administrative and comprised the units such as transport and supply companies, technical, commissariat, field police and medical troops.

PANZER GRENADIER DIVISION (Armoured Infantry)

These were originally *Infanterie Divisionen (Motorisiert)* but following the realisation that these needed strengthening to perform their intended role most were upgraded to semi-armoured status and renamed Panzer Grenadiers. A detailed breakdown of the units in a typical division is shown in Fig. 6. Basically it was intended to be parallel to the armoured division but with only a close-support tank abteilung – later replaced by an assault gun abteilung – and with its infantry component stronger and entirely motorised. In practice, especially during the later years of the war, it tended to be well below establishment and to have a high proportion of captured and other ersatz vehicles. There were normally six (SS sometimes nine) infantry Abteilungen.

INFANTRY DIVISION (Infanterie)

Infantry Divisions formed the bulk of the German army and initially comprised three infantry Regiments of three Abteilungen each, together with the normal supporting units – recce, signals, artillery, anti-tank, engineer and divisional services. They could be 'motorised' or 'horse-drawn', the latter being far the more common especially as the war went on. In either case they were, in effect, similar to the normal British infantry Division in that transport was restricted to supply and HQ elements, possibly with a small transport pool, the infantry companies being transported by train or GHQ pool transport if a long move was required. The recce abteilung, although so called by British sources, was often in reality no such thing. Known to the German army by various titles such as the '*Fusilier Bataillon*', '*Divisions Bataillon*', or '*Jaeger* (light infantry) Bataillon*', it was intended to perform as a mobile reserve and therefore included horsed or cyclist companies together with a mechanised heavy company which included anti-tank guns. It might even be formed largely by selection from others of the Division's units.

Indeed it was a feature of such Divisions that heavy weapons were even more decentralized than in Panzer units, each infantry regiment having its own anti-tank company. The Signals unit was equipped mainly with field telephone equipment in keeping with the intended static role of the Division and the artillery regiment had three field artillery abteilungen, each with twelve 10·5cm gun-howitzers, and a medium abteilung with eight 15cm gun howitzers and four 10cm guns. Anti aircraft protection was provided by a 2cm gun company in the divisional anti-tank Abteilung. This started the war with 3·7cm guns, was later issued with various 4·7cm and 5cm equipments either

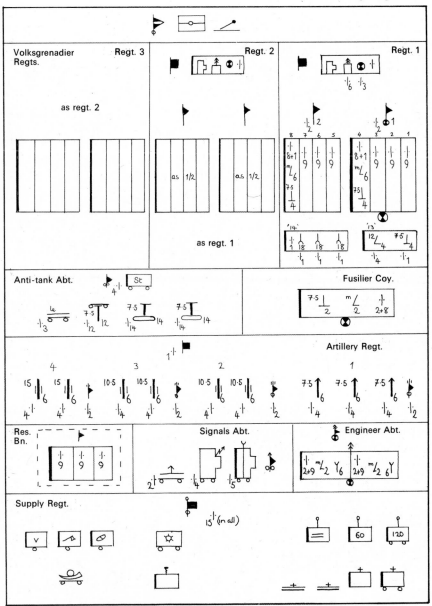

FIG 9 VOLKSGRENADIER DIVISION

towed or SP as they became available, and towards the end had a theoretical establishment of two 7·5cm gun companies and the 2cm gun company. The 7·5cm gun units could be SP or towed. The engineer Battalion was partly motorised and again organised as a strong infantry unit which included flame-throwers.

At the beginning of 1944 it was realised that the constant drain on manpower meant that many of these Divisions were under strength, and the more realistic *Infanterie Division 1944 Typ* establishment was adopted. This, while retaining most support units at only slightly reduced strength, reduced the rifle regiments to two Abteilungen each and the artillery regiment to two field and one medium Abteilung. At the same time anti-tank protection was improved, the regimental companies getting three 7·5cm guns each with a big allotment of infantry anti-tank projectors, and the small 5cm mortar was officially replaced at platoon level with a short 8·1cm pattern. Although having very little motor transport indeed, these Divisions were less unwieldy than the old ones and conserved manpower to some extent.

MOUNTAIN DIVISIONS (Gebirgs Divisionen):

The mountain Divisions stemmed from their predecessors of the First World War, and were in general well-equipped and elite formations. They were organised as infantry divisions and a fairly standard establishment is given in Fig. 10; in practice this was often varied according to where the Division was operating. Inevitably it had a high proportion of pack and horse transport while its support weapons were lighter than normal and designed for easy breakdown into manageable loads. The artillery regiment for example was equipped mainly with 7·5cm guns, its medium abteilung having 10·5cm weapons in place of 15cm ones. The only fully mechanised units in most divisions were the bridging columns of the engineer unit, but this was not really a great dis-advantage when one considers the type of terrain in which they were expected to operate.

LIGHT DIVISIONS (Leichte Divisionen) AND LIGHT IN-FANTRY DIVISIONS (Jaeger Divisionen):

The original four light Divisions (le Div 1–4) were formed in 1937–8 as fast, highly mobile, semi-mechanised formations – the modern equivalent to the old cavalry. No standard establishment appears to have been issued since they differed widely from each other but in general they were supposed to include:

(i) A Panzer Abteilung of three light companies with supporting troops. These were intended to be equipped with the specially designed Pzkw II Ausführung D and E tanks (see p.64) but in practice it appears that the bulk of these went to the independent Panzer Regiment 8 and the Divisional abteilungen had lorries and lightly armoured machine-gun cars.

(ii) One or two cavalry rifle regiments (*Reiter Regimenten*), organised under the old cavalry terminology into battalions (*Battaillone*) and squadrons (*Schwadrone*) rather than abteilungen and kompanien. Initially each regiment had two or three rifle battalions each typically of three horsed rifle squadrons with supporting motorised troops consisting of a machine gun squadron, a light

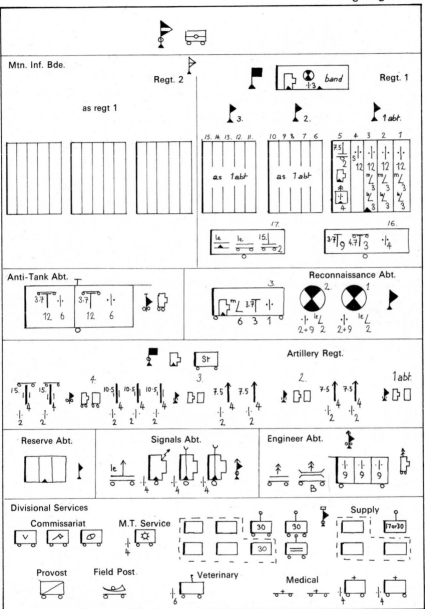

FIG 10 MOUNTAIN DIVISION

infantry gun squadron, an anti tank platoon (zug) and a light supply column. Nos 1 and 3 Divisions had one regiment and a motorcycle battalion each, Divisions 2 and 4 had two cavalry regiments.

(iii) Either a motorised recce battalion or a full Regiment, with armoured cars and a balanced tail of support troops as in the rifle regiments.

(iv) A small two-abteilung motorised artillery regiment with 24, 10·5cm gun howitzers.

(v) A four-company anti-tank abteilung with 36, 3·7cm guns and 12, 2cm flak guns.

(vi) A motorised engineer *battaillon* with two infantry companies, a Type K or B bridging column (see p. 118) and a light column.

(vii) Normal divisional services, all motorised.

It was originally intended to provide the cavalry units with highly efficient and well-armed half-track carriers but although prototypes were built, production was never undertaken. The Divisions were in any case anachronistic in the Blitzkrieg concept and from October 1939 on they were quickly converted into Panzer Divisions 6–9, all being so treated by mid-1940. Pz Regiment 8 formed the basis of another Panzer Division.

The name 'Light Division' was, however, revived at the end of 1940 when four infantry Divisions, 97, 99, 100, 101, were refitted for use mainly in Russia and the Balkans. These were not to the earlier pattern, their establishment being a cross between the normal horse-drawn infantry Division and a mountain Division, but with a considerable increase in motorised support transport. The 8th and 28th Infantry Divisions are said to have been similarly equipped during the winter of 1941–2.

As part of the morale-building propaganda, the designation of these units was changed to *Jaeger Divisionen* at the end of June 1942 and early in 1943 a further four infantry formations were 'elevated' to the same status (104, 114, 117–8), although, since they were intended for use in Greece and the Balkans, their establishment was more like that of a regular mountain Division; they were sometimes known as *Gebirgs Jaeger Divisionen*, the term apparently also being applied occasionally to regular mountain units.

Meanwhile, back in early 1941, the name '*Leichte Division*' was used also for three special formations. The first was 5th Light Division, formed from the remnants of 5th Infantry Division in January, for service in Africa. It was completely non-standard to any previous establishment (see p. 167) and had a short life, being reconstituted as 21st Panzer Division in July 1941. It was followed however by the similar but weaker '*Afrika*' light motorised division formed new from a Zbv Division staff (see p. 52), which soon became the famous 90th Light Division equipped virtually to full panzer grenadier standards and reconstituted as such after the Tunis disaster. Lastly, in May–June 1942, 164 Infantry Division was reformed as the 164 Leichte Afrika Division, basically as a motorised infantry unit. As with 90th Light, it had a special establishment and eventually became a panzer grenadier unit.

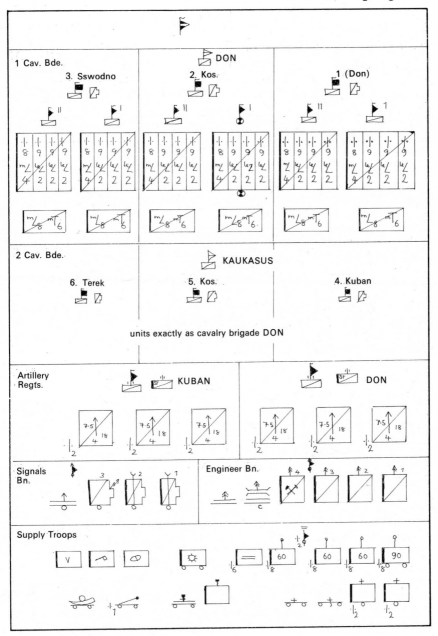

FIG 11 KOSAKEN DIVISION

CAVALRY DIVISIONS (KAVALLERIE DIVISIONEN):
The position regarding German cavalry (ie genuine mounted troops) is not entirely clear since it was very little used in the West and, hence, there is little Intelligence information. At the outbreak of war there were in existence the four Leichte Divisionen with their mounted rifle regiments and also 1st Cavalry Brigade. This unit after participating in the Polish campaign attached to a Panzer group, was raised to divisional status in time for the 1940 French campaign. As a partly mechanised mobile Division it then fought in Russia until the end of 1941 when it was converted into 24th Panzer Division.

It would appear, however, that there were always cavalry units operating on the Russian front after 1941. Certainly the Waffen SS had their *SS Cavalry Division* (the *SS Division Florian Geyer*), with mounted infantry Regiments, and mounted regiments were operating as autonomous units with the army during 1942 and 1943. In May 1943 six regiments were combined to form the Army *Kosaken Division* (Cossack Division) patterned after the Russian cavalry and having largely horse-drawn support units roughly equivalent to those in a mountain division but without anti-tank protection. This (Fig. 11) was a true cavalry Division and operated as such until it was taken over by the SS at the end of 1944 and split up to form the nucleus of XV SS Kavallerie Korps (2 Divisions); these two appear to have been organised similarly to mobile infantry divisions so far as the war situation allowed. For a period, until it was annihilated there was also a Hungarian Cavalry Division in the order of battle. The cavalry units taken to form Kosaken division were obviously missed since, by February 1944, at least three strong cavalry regiments were operating with Army Group Centre. Between February and May 1944 these were organised into the basis of 3 *and* 4 *Kavallerie Brigaden* each composed of two, two-battalion regiments with strong and partly motorised supporting units (Fig. 12). These were obviously a means of providing mobile striking forces under Russian conditions where the horse had advantages even over motor transport at times, and were mounted infantry rather than true cavalry. With the 'loss' of Kosaken Division they were both upgraded to Divisional status from the end of February 1945 by the addition of appropriate Divisional services units. At the war's end there were two army and four SS Cavalry Divisions officially in the field with a fifth SS one forming.

VOLKSGRENADIER DIVISIONS (lit: People's Rifle Divisions):
These were fairly low grade units formed from September 1944 on, after Himmler became C-in-C of the *Ersatzarmee*. As with so many items in 1944–5, the name was political in origin to increase morale and the Divisions had close links with the SS – their troops were said to be interchangeable though there is no evidence of this. They were usually built from the remains of line infantry units – eg 6th Inf Div, after virtual destruction by the Russians, rose anew as 6th Volksgrenadier. They were organised as infantry Divisions with a reduction in personnel and an increase in automatic firepower. (Fig. 9.) The main differences from the 1944 Infantry Division pattern were:
   (i) The recce element was reduced to a Fusilier company.
   (ii) One infantry regiment was designated 'bicycle' (*rad*, or *radfahrer*), having one Abteilung equipped with these machines as a mobile reserve.

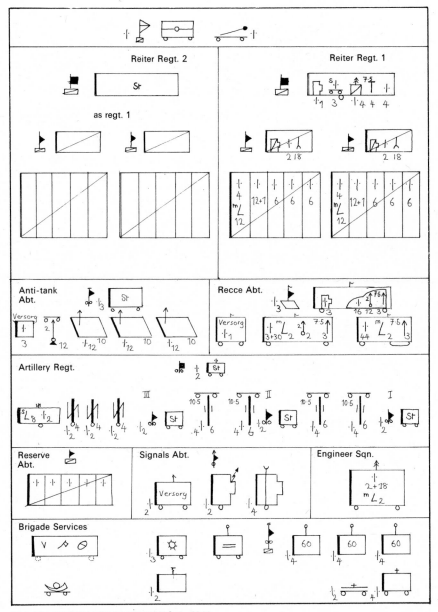

FIG 12 CAVALRY BRIGADE late 1944

(iii) Bazooka or Panzerfaust companies replaced the infantry regimental anti-tank gun companies.

(iv) The artillery regiment had one 7·5cm gun abteilung with eight guns, two light Abteilungen each with twelve 10·5cm gun-howitzers, and a medium abteilung of twelve 15cm gun-howitzers, all heavier guns being organised in six-gun batteries.

(v) Anti-tank and engineer units were reduced in strength.

(vi) Supply was simplified into Abteilung supply columns and a single Divisional supply regiment which incorporated all the normal divisional services except the military police who came directly under Division HQ.

These divisions were formed at a stage of the war when both manpower and material was becoming scarce and it is unlikely that many were formed at full strength; nonetheless some 50 in all were formed or rebuilt from other formations before the war ended. They were normally equipped with horse-drawn transport.

SCHATTEN DIVISIONEN (lit: SHADOW DIVISIONS)

These, hardly mentioned in Intelligence summaries, were largely decoy units set up at intervals to deceive the enemy into thinking the Germans were stronger than they in fact were. Exact organisation varied but in general they comprised an HQ, a weak infantry regiment with minimum services and a small amount of field artillery – sufficient to make a show. All were named, either for code or propaganda purposes, and were either retained in home areas or sent to 'safe' occupied regions to release more battleworthy units. They appeared in the Order of Battle as infantry Divisions.

ASSAULT DIVISIONS (STURM DIVISIONEN)

This was a morale-building name given to a few low-grade infantry Divisions having reduced numbers but an increase in short range firepower. They can be considered as prototypes for the later Volksgrenadier units.

Luftwaffe Units Fighting with the Army

Like Heinrich Himmler and the SS, Hermann Goering, C-in-C of the Air Force, had what was almost his own private army formed from specialist units such as the paratroops and from redundant personnel combed out during the last years of the war. The specialist paratroops were high quality and when fighting as paratroops were under Luftwaffe control. Otherwise all units were controlled by the army, although with some interference. The only significant armoured unit was the *Hermann Goering Division*, which started as a panzer grenadier unit and graduated to a full Panzer Division before being incorporated in a so-called Panzer Korps. It was a good-quality unit and functioned as part of the army though always listed as a Luftwaffe formation in the order of battle.

LUFTWAFFE FELD DIVISIONEN

These were formed from late 1942 on when, as a result of manpower shortages, it was decided to comb-out redundant ground personnel of the air-force and to form them into infantry Divisions mainly for static roles. Some twenty

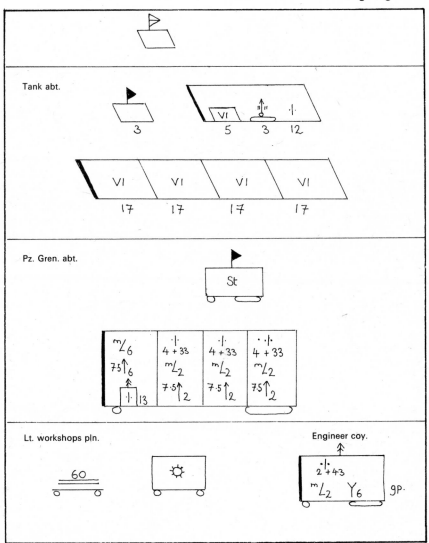

FIG 13 PANZER BRIGADE Typ 1944

Tank abt.

Pz. Gren. abt.

Lt. workshops pln.

Engineer coy.

Divisions in all were formed, with a theoretical establishment similar to a 1944-type horse-drawn infantry Division, with the following differences:

  (i)   A recce company replaced the recce battalion.
  (ii) The artillery regiment had 7·5cm guns instead of 10·5cm gun-howitzers.
  (iii) A full Luftwaffe AA Abteilung of eight 8·8cm guns and twelve 2cm guns was included.
  (iv) All support units were reduced in size.

Since in practice the Divisions were improvised very quickly some did not reach even this establishment and were used as fortress troops. In practice they came under local army command but as with other 'private' forces there was always interference from their former owners.

AIRBORNE TROOPS

These were divided into two categories: air landing troops and parachute troops.

AIR LANDING TROOPS: These were in theory any army units that had been trained in rapid emplaning and deplaning. They were taken as required from normal infantry Divisions for specific operations and were intended to follow up once parachute troops had secured a landing ground. 22nd Infantry Division and possibly other units had special weapons allocations to meet this specific need.

PARACHUTE TROOPS (*Fallschirmjaeger*): These were *Luftwaffe* formations and when employed on airborne operations came under Luftwaffe operational control. Initially *Fliegerkorps XI* was organised as an airborne corps providing several parachute Divisions together with supporting corps units such as AA and machine gun abteilungen, Engineer and Signals units and various other support formations. The main fighting forces were provided by the parachute Divisions each of which consisted of:

  (i)   A Recce company or battalion.
  (ii) Three parachute rifle regiments, each of three Abteilungen with supporting Infantry gun (recoilless) and anti-tank companies.
  (iii) A Parachute artillery regiment of two Abteilungen, with a total of twelve 10·5cm recoilless guns.
  (iv) A parachute anti-tank Abteilung usually equipped with 5cm airborne pattern guns.
  (v)   Engineer and signals units.

Services were restricted to transport and supply since it was not envisaged that the Divisions would fight for prolonged periods. These Divisions were elite formations and even after airborne operations were discontinued were kept together as highly effective shock troops to be used in a fire-brigade capacity. Their main disadvantage was the absence of heavy weapons. They did not always fight as Divisions, some being reorganised as infantry brigades (eg Parachute Brigade Ramcke which fought in North Africa).

The above were the main fighting divisions of the German Army but there were others which should be mentioned briefly, although they were usually only

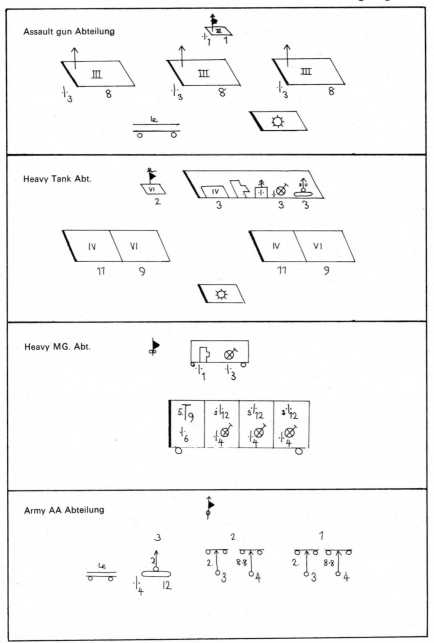

FIG 14   EXAMPLES OF ARMY UNITS

administrative staffs controlling assorted units. They were:

Sicherungs Division (lit: security Division) controlling military police and provost services in an area.

Coast Defence Division: Staff controlling assorted units.

Grenzwach (frontier) Division: Staff controlling frontier patrol units.

Divisions Nummer	
Zbv Division	Basically Divisional staffs in existence and used to con-
Reserve Division	trol various activities. Examples of all were from time
Feldausbildungs Division	to time used as the basis of normal fighting formations.

Army and Corps Troops

As in any army of the period, higher formations always retained special units of both fighting and support troops which could be used as a central reserve or allocated to Divisions for some particular operation. In the German army these did include general purpose units such as machine gun companies, army anti-aircraft units (*heeresflak*) and assault engineers but they were mostly collections of heavier or more specialised equipment than that allotted to Divisions. Thus they included heavy artillery, heavy (Tiger) tank battalions, 8·8cm and later 12·8cm anti-tank units, assault gun batteries and flame-throwing tanks besides multifarious varieties of engineer units. The fighting weapons were often grouped into Brigades of which the most well-known was the 1944-pattern armoured Brigade shown in Fig. 13. Most smoke and chemical warfare equipment, together with its associated decontamination units, also came under GHQ control as did batteries of heavy multiple mortars and rocket projectors. Some of the more interesting are shown in Fig. 14.

It may be worth noting here that most heavy flak units were Luftwaffe operated and controlled but they could be allocated to army tactical control for specific defensive operations. They then formed a very effective addition to anti-tank strength since they included quantities of dual-purpose 8·8cm guns.

4
Basic
Tactics

Every army has its basic tactics – policies and plans for triumphing on the battlefield – and every army constantly modifies them in detail or on a large scale as circumstances change. This chapter describes the bare outlines of German army tactics in the 1939–45 war.

From the war's outset, German General Staff policy taught that only the offensive achieved success and that the defensive should be employed only as a holding operation or to provide a more secure base for future offensive operations. This principle, embodied in the tactical doctrine of the *Blitzkrieg* (lit: lightning war) was clearly demonstrated during the first years of World War 2 and dominated German military thinking and action up to about 1943. It was only when first the Russians and then the Allies had succeeded in stopping the German rush and in wearing away the air superiority on which the Blitzkrieg depended, that this doctrine was superseded. It is a measure of the tactical flexibility of the Army's 'local' commanders that in the field it was able to adapt on a large scale to a policy of delaying-action defence and to do so largely without air cover. It was greatly helped, much to the allies surprise, by the very considerable qualities of responsibilities and initiative possessed by the junior officers and NCOs; to planners brought up on the 1914–18 concept of a German army having no initiative in the lower ranks it was a particular shock to find that this no longer applied.

Unfortunately for the Germans, this flexibility was not matched by the High Command, especially the more politically biased appointments; army commanders were often forbidden any flexibility! In particular Hitler himself, often such a driving force when the army was victorious, became a severe liability when it was forced to the defensive. His constant insistence on the holding of ground to the last man and on the launching of old-style counter attacks that were impracticable in changed circumstances cost the army dear both in men and material. The basic field tactics within this framework can be divided into three main parts:

Reconnaissance

This task is common to all armies until they meet in battle. The Germans divided it roughly into: Operational Reconnaissance (*Operative Aufklarung*) which they considered as general long range observation, mainly by air; Tactical Reconnaissance (*Taktische Aufklarung*) which was carried out 15–20 miles in advance of an attacking force by motorised or armoured units specially organised for the task; and Battle Reconnaissance (*Gefechts Aufklarung*) which was close range reconnaissance as a Division or similar force moved in to engage an enemy. The latter pattern was the most important and, according to the principle whereby armoured units made the first thrust, was entrusted wherever possible to the armoured reconnaissance Abteilungen of the armoured Divisions. The 'standard' patrol consisted of three armoured cars operating on a narrow front and providing mutual observation and covering fire. In practice the lead vehicle was often used as a decoy, being driven close to suspected enemy positions and then withdrawing rapidly once it had exposed these by drawing their fire; this tactic was much aided by the double-ended design of standard German armoured cars (see p. 75), and since they were not expected to fight to nearly the same extent as allied formations, the vehicles were lighter and faster than their allied equivalents.

Once contact was established it was normal practice to try to build up a local superiority in numbers, calling on the reserve armoured infantry of the battalion to enable scouting to be pushed forwards and enemy outposts to be driven in. Infantry as such were not normally expected to undertake offensive reconnaissance since the Infantry Divisions were intended only to consolidate and to mop up, but in specialised circumstances (eg mountain work or in other difficult terrain) they were used. In such cases, fighting patrols of up to 15–20 men – but more often 7–8 – were sent out in World War 1 fashion. They were armed mainly with automatic and semi-automatic weapons and were not expected to engage in serious and prolonged fighting. Their duty was to take prisoners if possible and to report. The practice of using infantry naturally became more common when the army was forced permanently on the defensive, and infantry Divisions then often had specialist bicycle or mounted units for mobile reconnaissance work.

Offensive

The basic concept of the offensive for the German army was to encircle and destroy the enemy, using local superiority in armour, fire power and surprise. The Germans quite rightly distrusted the classical massed frontal attack, considering it expensive in both men and material, and also the most difficult way to achieve success. Where possible (eg in the 1940 French campaign) they preferred to strike at a flank and then encircle the enemy. Where a front had to be pierced they employed what was known as the *Schwerpunkt* (lit: centre of gravity; thence point of maximum effort) concept. (Fig. 15.)

This required surprise since it postulated a penetration of the enemy on a narrow front by superior and fast-moving forces, while diversionary attacks on adjoining sectors prevented the enemy moving up reinforcements. The penetration was then extended straight forward as a breakthrough with the object of overrunning the enemy's rear echelons and so threatening his communications that he would have to retire his whole front. Its success, after the initial penetration, depended on being able to seal off the flanks of the breakthrough to protect German communications and on having a powerful central reserve that could be quickly switched to exploit an opportunity. The form shown in Fig. 15 was often known to the Germans as *Keil und Kessel* (Wedge and Cauldron) since if it worked the opposing forces could be first shattered and then trapped

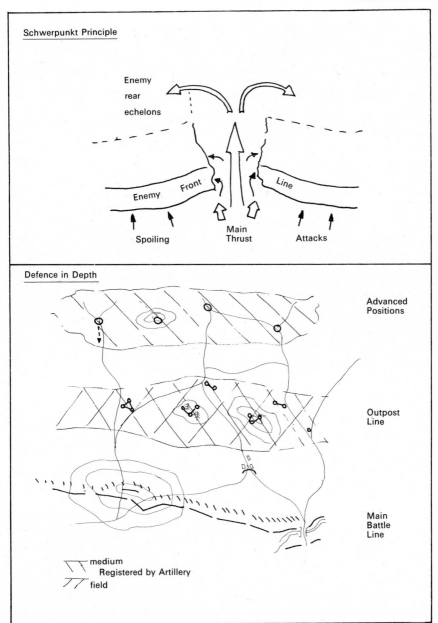

Schwerpunkt Principle

Enemy
rear
echelons

Enemy Front Line

Spoiling   Main   Attacks
              Thrust

Defence in Depth

Advanced
Positions

Outpost
Line

Main
Battle
Line

medium
Registered by Artillery
field

FIG 15 ATTACK AND DEFENCE

10. The might of the Wehrmacht: Tiger 1 (Ausf. E) tanks on guard in the Brenner Pass. The tanks appear to be new and in basic yellow. Note the infantry camouflaged shelter quarters (see p. 128) combined to form bivouacs. (MH 6296)

in a 'cauldron' from which they could not escape. The earlier Russian front campaigns are classic examples of the successful use of that tactic on a large scale.

In detail, the original concept was that of Captain Liddel Hart's 'expanding torrent' – a massed tank breakthrough, supported by aircraft, that protected its flanks by its own speed and by the confusion it caused. Once the initial surprise had worn off, however, and with a decline in air superiority, the concept was modified to allow an attacking force to protect its own flanks.

Until the end of the war, armoured formations were expected to spearhead such attacks but against prepared positions a more cautious approach was progressively adopted. An attack was normally on a Divisional basis at least and theoretically comprised a unified force of tanks, armoured and motorised infantry, and self-propelled assault guns. Originally, massed artillery barrages were envisaged but in practice the Germans were rarely able to concentrate their guns as well as the allies could, and improvements in camouflage in any case meant that enemy positions could often not be identified until close combat was joined. Thus even the Divisional artillery Regiments were often decentralised, a substitute being provided to some extent by multi-barrelled mortars and close-support assault weapons.

The basic scheme was that the tanks would attack initially in two or more often three waves, with armoured infantry in half-track carriers sandwiched between them and with SP anti-tank and assault guns on the flanks; these were

56

effectively dual purpose since all German guns could fire both high explosive and armour-piercing shot. The first wave took the brunt of the fighting, thrusting through to the enemy anti-tank and infantry positions, while the second wave and infantry gave covering fire and then dealt with any remaining opposition. The third wave with supporting motorised infantry then came in to establish the breakthrough and guard the attack's flanks while the remains of the first two waves thrust straight for the enemy's artillery positions and struck at his rear. Enemy tanks, it should be noted, were supposed specifically to be engaged by the accompanying mobile assault guns and specialised tank destroyers (Panzerjaeger or Jagdpanzer).

The massed infantry attack was by no means so common although, when used, it was on the same basis. In detail, where possible, penetration was to be achieved by infiltration tactics linked with the use of special assault squads (*Stosstruppe*) to overcome key strongpoints. Much greater emphasis was placed on artillery and mortar support and in principle assault howitzers were to be used in large numbers, engaging enemy support weapons over open sights if required. Special assault gun brigades were formed for this purpose although, as the war went on, their massed use became less and less common. The Germans were extremely adept at infiltration, which was often very successful as much because of the confusion it caused as for any other reason, but once they reverted to massed frontal infantry attacks – as they did for instance at Anzio – their effectiveness was greatly decreased.

Defence

Defensive operations were originally envisaged as holding situations pending resumption of the offensive and laying great stress on immediate and violent counter attacks; the principle was to catch a presumably rather disorganised enemy before he could reform after his attack. After 1943, however, it became obvious that a more general defensive posture was needed and the principle of defence in depth was redeveloped, using experience gained especially on the Russian front.

The principle was to have three main defence areas. First came a series of advanced positions some 5–7000 yards ahead of the main defence zone. These, within range of the medium artillery, were manned by light mobile units whose main task was to make the enemy deploy too early and if possible in the wrong sector. They were not supposed to hold out at all costs but were to slip away when their job was done, leading the enemy on to the next line of defence.

This, which might be called the outpost position, was in a zone 2–2500 yards ahead of the main defences and covered by the light field artillery. It consisted of individual prepared positions sited so far as possible to give each other mutual support and manned by infantry units, support weapons and anti-tank gun teams. Infantry weapons were normally the longer range ones – machine guns and rifles – and if possible alternative positions were prepared in advance so that quick moves could be made from one to another to confuse the enemy; the Germans were particularly adept at rapid and efficient transfer of mortars, thus avoiding easy location by enemy observers. As far as possible, all outpost positions were selected to facilitate unobserved withdrawal by their occupants and were often registered by the German artillery so that their occupation could be denied to the enemy.

Finally there was the main battle zone (*Hauptkampflinie*) consisting, where a stabilised line was in being, of connected strong points. These, sited on reverse slopes if possible, had an all-round field of fire, were protected at least in principle by thick belts of wire and mines, and were manned by riflemen and machine gunners backed by mortars and heavy weapons. It is of interest that unless they had plenty of time the Germans did not like building such points in woods because of the greater expenditure of effort, and that on rivers they liked to have defensive positions on the 'enemy' side thus making the river an integral part of their anti-tank defence. Perhaps more than in other armies the art of field camouflage* and the 'improvement' of natural obstacles to an enemy's advance were brought to a high pitch of perfection. Combined with the use of flashless propellant these often made quite lightly defended positions appear formidable, which considerably held up allied attacks.

In fact it is fair to say that, while they retained mobility, German forces were adept at the timely and unobtrusive withdrawal so that allied bombs and artillery barrages often fell harmlessly on empty trenches. Their army organisation and the high degree of tactical initiative instilled into the regular officer and NCO cadres also meant that 'ad hoc' formations could be quickly improvised from any odd units available to plug gaps in an emergency. These battlegroups (*kampfgruppen*) were a regular feature of German field tactics and could range from company-sized groups of infantry right up to divisional-sized combina-

---

*As opposed to deception camouflage to mislead the enemy.

11. And the rabble: A very improvised transport column, mainly of ex-Austrian equipment. The nearest vehicles are the peculiarly Austrian 'Mulus' wheel-and-track weapons carriers, the remainder appear to be impressed civilian vehicles. (STT 739)

tions of all arms; the Kampfgruppe Pieper, one of the units that spearheaded the Ardennes offensive in December 1944, was an excellent example of the latter, while a study of the fighting at Arnhem in Operation Market Garden gives a good glimpse of the ability to improvise in a sudden emergency.

Once the Germans were forced into a crust defence, however, as they were from late 1944 on, small tactical tricks could not save the day since lack of mobility meant (a) that a line had to hold until it was broken since it was difficult to provide a controlled withdrawal and (b) any reserve line had to be constructed at a considerable distance to ensure time for its completion.

5
Equipment

In the space of this book, it is possible only to describe in detail the standard equipment of the German army during World War 2. Readers will therefore not find more than superficial mention of:

(i)   Pre-war equipment used only in small quantities and early on in the war.

(ii)   Projected developments (eg the 180 tonne *Maus* tank) which existed only in prototype or drawing forms.

(iii)   The fantastic variety of captured equipment that was pressed into service at various times. Only those foreign equipments that were 'standardised' in quantity are described.

So far as standard equipment was concerned, German quality varied. In battle armour, the development of specialised assault guns, and in anti-tank equipments, they were generally well in advance of contemporary allied design and practice, with the possible exception of the Russian T34 and Stalin tank series. In ordinary artillery they tended to lag behind, and in infantry weapons their showing was variable. Rifles and pistols were unexceptionable, mortars were average but very intelligently employed, and light automatic weapons were on the whole superior to their allied counterparts. The purpose-designed soft vehicles were probably as efficient as those of any other army but there were never enough of the standard vehicles to go round so that a most varied and ramshackle collection of sub-standard equipment had to be pressed into service.

For the purposes of this chapter, the numerous self-propelled weapons have been crudely divided into two categories. Purpose-designed weapons on standard chassis, normally with armoured fighting rooms, are classed as battle armour; improvisations in which guns were simply mounted on obsolete chassis with only light shielding for the crew are dealt with under the appropriate artillery section. Infantry weapons are covered in Chapter 6.

Battle Armour
(Panzerkampfwagen – Pzkw; Sturmgeschütze – Stu.G.; Jagdpanzer – Jagd.)
Note: panzer jaeger and other improvised self-propelled equipments will be found under 'Artillery'.

The early development of German battle armour stemmed from the development, during the late 1920s, of the Blitzkrieg concept. Unfortunately for the Germans it was not possible to conceal tank development in the same way as less conspicuous vehicles could be hidden – in civilian guise. Experiments were, however, carried out with the so-called light and heavy tractors, fully tracked

12. First real tank in the German armoury was the Pzkw II, here seen in its Ausf. F version. This is a regimental HQ vehicle, as can be seen from its turret markings (p. 151).   (MH 4134)

chassis that laid the foundations for the later standard patterns of tank (to become Pzkw III and IV). These commenced development in the early 1930s but it was obvious that interim types would be needed, if only for training. This in turn led to the development and production under various guises of two light tanks, the Pzkw I and II which, together with Czech machines assimilated from 1939 on, formed the main strength of the German Panzer Divisions for both the Polish and French campaigns. They were supplemented in 1940 and then supplanted by the standard battle tanks III, at first with a 3·7cm gun and then steadily upgunned; and IV which was at first envisaged as a close support weapon with a short 7·5cm gun. This latter machine proved so robust and versatile that, constantly uparmoured and upgunned, it remained the mainstay of the Panzer Divisions until the war's end. Meanwhile hard experience on the Russian front against the outstanding T34 tank had shown the need for rapid new developments. First the Type VI or Tiger heavy tank was introduced and then the lighter Panther. The latter was potentially the best tank produced by either side but, like the Tiger, it was pushed into production too soon and suffered from extended teething troubles. The final operational tank, the massive 76 tonne Tiger 2, was considered by allied experts at the time to be far too massive, although the Germans were even then experimenting with vehicles of over 100 tonnes. More recent developments in NATO and elsewhere have justified its concept but for its period it was too unwieldy and unreliable to be of great value.

Parallel with tank development, the Germans produced both improvised and purpose-designed assault weapons on standard tank chassis. The concept,

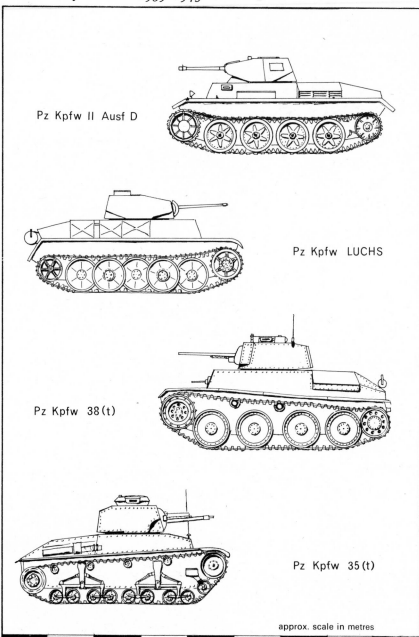

Pz Kpfw II Ausf D

Pz Kpfw LUCHS

Pz Kpfw 38 (t)

Pz Kpfw 35 (t)

approx. scale in metres

FIG 16   LIGHT TANKS

formulated and developed long before the allies had such weapons, was that by dispensing with a turret, a given tank chassis could mount a heavier gun than normal and be provided with thicker and better shaped frontal armour for close range work. The first assault gun was the Sturmgeschütz III, based on the Pzkw III chassis and mounting a short-barrelled 7·5cm gun for infantry co-operation work. It proved so successful that the concept was extended later both to the mounting of heavier close-support weapons and to the mounting of long-barrelled guns in similar housings. These were initially improvised – upgunned Stu.G III and Stu.G IV which could be used both for infantry support and as ersatz battle tanks. Later on, however, specialised Jagdpanzer (hunter-tanks) were developed on the Type IV, Panther and Tiger 2 chassis. These had well-designed sloped armour and usually carried bigger or longer guns than their tank equivalents; their specific task was to outgun and kill enemy tanks and, once again, they were ahead of their time.

For those who wish to go into detail there are many excellent books on various tanks (see Bibliography). These brief notes are intended only to give a general picture of each major type. (It may be noted here that the common historical practice of referring to types as 'marks' (eg Mark IV) is not really accurate. The German designation is 'Tank IV' which may be better trans-lated as 'Type'. The 'Marks' are really the various models (Ausführung) of each major Type – eg Panzer IV, Ausf. G.)

*Pzkpfw I (Sdkfz 101) (PL 1): This vehicle was the result of a competition for a light armoured fighting vehicle in the 5–10 tonne range and was developed by Krupp under the codename '*Landwirtschaftschlepper*' or LaS (industrial tractor). It was basically a lightly armoured, rear-engined, machine-gun carrier

*Alternative designation abbreviation was Pzkw.

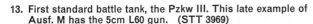

13. First standard battle tank, the Pzkw III. This late example of Ausf. M has the 5cm L60 gun. (STT 3969)

with two MG 13s in a revolving turret. 150 of the first model (Ausführung A) were built in 1934–5 and this was replaced in production from 1935 on by the more powerful and slightly larger Ausführung B. Some 1500 were in service by 1939 and they served as combat tanks in both Poland and France, not being finally retired until late 1941 when the chassis went out of production. The only serious developments were a small production batch of an air-landing variant (40 only) and an experimental batch with increased armour – which the basic chassis could not cope with. Surplus chassis were used as the basis for munitions carriers, tractors, stop-gap self-propelled guns and as command vehicles (*panzerbefehlswagen*).

Pzkw II (Sdkfz 121. PL 12): General Guderian, the most perceptive of the German Panzer experts, realised that the Pzkw I – little more than a training device – would not be sufficient, and MAN designed a further 'industrial tractor' – LaS100 – this time in the 10 tonne bracket and mysteriously capable of sprouting a 2cm gun and an MG34 machine gun in a revolving turret. Again the first models (Ausf a1–3, and b) introduced in 1935 and 1936 had only rifle-proof armour but Ausf. B had its frontal armour increased to 30mm and Ausf.C had an improved suspension. This latter was the backbone of the Panzer Divisions in 1940 and, along with its simplified and uparmoured derivative the Ausf.F which appeared in 1940, was used right into 1942 as a Reconnaissance tank by HQ platoons of tank battalions. Ausführung D and E were different: They, under the designation LaS138, combined the hull and turret

14. Mainstay of the Panzers, the Pzkw IV. Typical of the later versions
is this Ausf. G with the 7·5cm L48 gun but without additional skirt
armour. (MH 4138)

of the model C with a Christie-type suspension having four large intermediate wheels without return rollers; this made for a higher road speed but reduced cross-country performance. They were intended for use in the tank battalions of the Light Divisions and, when these units were converted to Panzer Divisions, were used as the basis for self-propelled guns. They were all – about 250 – built in 1937–8. As with Pzkw 1, redundant chassis, and others made available by stopping production of the battle tank, were used as the basis for various SP gun mountings.

Pzkpfw 35 (t): By 1939 the 'standard tanks' were still not available in quantity but the Czech army, taken over during the German occupation, had two fairly robust and modern tank designs in service. The first was the LTM 35, taken into 6th Panzer Division as the Pzkw 35 (t). 167 examples of this vehicle were acquired but, although it mounted a 3·7cm gun it was not entirely satisfactory, having riveted armour, a high silhouette and an old design of suspension (Fig. 16). The redundant chassis were later used as artillery munitions carriers and tractors.

Pzkpfw 38 (t): The other Czech design, the TNHP-8, was, however, an excellent chassis, kept in production as an interim battle tank until 1942 – at one period in 1940 it accounted for a quarter of German tank strength. It mounted a 3·7cm gun and a 7·9mm machine gun in a revolving turret as a battle tank (Fig. 16) and, when superseded in mid-1942 the hull was used as the basis for various SP guns such as the Marder III (Fig. 21). Production of

15. Perhaps the deadliest medium tank of WW2, this late production PANTHER, Ausf. G, shows the way in which identity numbers were changed and also the Zimmerit anti-magnetic coating. (MH 4142)

16. The final operational tank, a Tiger 2 (*Koenigstiger*), with the production turret and an 8·8cm L70 gun. Here again the Zimmerit coating and, unusually, a turret cross can be seen. (PC 409)

these did not stop until May 1944, when all available production was com-mandeered for the *Hetzer*, a light but extremely effective jagdpanzer design (Pl. 20). Classed as a panzerjaeger (tank destroyer), probably because it was intended for issue to the defensive anti-tank units of infantry Divisions, it was fast (40kph), had 60mm frontal armour with a well-shaped fighting hull, and mounted a 7·5cm PaK 38/L48 gun with a roof-mounted machine gun for local defence. It was so highly thought of that even after the war it was pro-duced for several years for both the Czech and Swiss armies. Much smaller quantities of a flamethrowing variant and armoured recovery vehicle (*berge-panzer*) were also produced on this chassis during late 1944 and 1945.

Pzkpfw III (Sdkfz 141): This vehicle, in the 20 tonne range, was intended to be the main battle tank of the German army and was developed from 1935 on by Daimler Benz under the disguise name of *Zugführerwagen* (platoon com-mander's vehicle). Even at the start there was some argument about the size of gun to be used and although a 3·7cm gun was fitted initially, to allow standardisation with the contemporary anti-tank gun, the turret ring was made big enough to take a 5cm weapon if required. The development variants com-prised Ausführungen A, B, C, and D, to which standard, all previous models were modified, but the first standard production model was Ausführung E of 1939 vintage. Adopted officially as the Sdkfz 141, it had the definitive running gear with torsion bar suspension, 30mm armour all round and a turreted 3·7cm gun with an MG34 mounted coaxially. Some 349 were in service for the 1940 French campaign but even then upgunning with the 5cm L/42 tank gun was in progress, and Models F, G, and H followed rapidly.

The provision of the L/42 gun was something of a blunder and it was only on Hitler's insistence that the more powerful L/60 version was fitted to all

66

17. An example of special armoured vehicles: The *Bergepanther* tank
recovery vehicle on Panther chassis. (IWM)

tanks from 1941 on (Ausf. J-L) including all reconditioned vehicles. Ausführung M (Pl. 13) was produced from May 1942 and from the end of that year
examples were refitted with the old 7·5cm L/24 gun for close support work as
'ersatz' for Assault guns, this weapon being standard fitment on the final
variant, N. It is interesting to note that the conditions on the Russian front had
so changed that the roles of the battle tanks – with inadequate armour – and the
more heavily armoured and gunned assault weapons on the same chassis had
been reversed. Production of the battle tank in fact terminated in August 1943
to release chassis for assault guns but tank variants were in use until the end of
the war, particularly in those areas where modern allied armour was not likely
to be encountered (eg Denmark; the Balkans).

Apart from the constant development of the basic tank, important variations
were the 52 examples of Ausführung E that were specially converted for deep
wading up to 13 feet in preparation for the invasion of England; the fitting of
side and turret skirting plates from 1943 on as protection against hollow-charge
projectiles; and the conversion of 100 model Ms into flamethrowers with the
flame gun replacing the normal 5cm gun. Other variants included command
tanks from 1939 on (especially on the Ausführung D), some with dummy
armament; artillery observation tanks (*beobachtungspanzer*); armoured recovery
vehicle (*Bergepanzer*); and the so-called *Schlepper III*, an improvised load
carrier on a Type III chassis which was used among other things for carrying
ammunition and bridging equipment. *The Sturmgeschütz III* (Sdkfz 142) or
Stu.G III was a radical adaptation of the basic chassis dating from a 1936
requirement for infantry close support vehicles. It was in effect a turretless tank
having an armoured fighting compartment with thick, sloped frontal armour
and mounting a short 7·5cm L/24 gun with only limited traverse. Five proto-

types took part in the 1940 French campaign and series production started in July 1940, the first five models (A–E) having only minor differences. In September 1941, Hitler personally ordered it to be uparmed as the Ausführung F, first with a 7·5cm L/43 gun and then with the very effective 7·5cm kwk L/48 (Pl. 18). Increasingly these vehicles were diverted from the artillery to long range assault gun and anti-tank roles but about 1 in 10 were built with 10·5cm L/42 gun howitzers for the original close-support role and some were built without armament as munitions carriers. A project to mount the heavy infantry gun sIG 33 in an open fighting compartment was called off in favour of the Type IV Brummbär (qv) after only twelve had been built.

Pzkpfw iv (Pl. 14) (Sdkfz 161): This tank was developed in parallel with Type III under the code name '*Battailonsführerwagen*' and its basic features were finalised on the first production version, Ausführung A, which appeared in 1936–7. Conceived for the infantry tank or close support role, production was initially quite low although successive improvements, especially in armour thickness, led to Models B–E appearing by late 1939. Its real turning point came with the introduction of Ausführung F2 in late 1941, with the long 7·5 L/43 gun, and the subsequent Ausf.G with the L/48 gun. These showed such a marked improvement in firepower over existing tanks that they were selected as the standard tanks of the Panzer Divisions and great efforts were made to maximise production. After the G, only detail improvements in frontal armour (up to 85mm) and in the addition of skirting plates were made, the H

18. 'Typical' assault weapon: the purpose-designed Stug. III. This example with the long 7·5cm gun shows clearly the cupola, machine gun shield (folded) and the limited traverse available for the gun. (MH 9064)

and J models remaining in production until the end of the war. Various examples of Ausführung H were used with only minor modifications as command vehicles (*Befehlswagen IV*).

Pz IV ASSAULT GUNS AND OTHER VARIANTS: The basic Type IV chassis as an extremely reliable and robust vehicle, was also used for a wide variety of other duties. Most important were the various assault guns: from 1943–on it was built as an assault gun with almost identical superstructure to the Stug III and mounting the L/48 gun (Sdkfz 163); this was frequently used, on the Russian front especially, as a substitute battle tank. It was replaced in production early in 1944 by the *Jagdpanzer IV* (Sdkfz 162), a purpose-designed tank destroyer with low silhouette, well-sloped armour and the 7·5cm PaK 39/L48 in a limited traverse mounting with the so-called *Saukopf* (pigs head) cast mantlet (Fig. 17). From August 1944 this was supplemented in small numbers by the Jagdpanzer IV variant with the 7·5cm StuK L/70, equivalent to the Panther tank gun. This proved fairly effective but was somewhat unmanoeuvrable and was not favoured. The L/48 was quite competent enough to knock out any tank of the Western allies! Attempts were also made to combine the best elements of the Type III and Type IV chassis as the *Geschutzwagen III/IV* (gun carriage III/IV). Both this and the standard chassis were used as mounts for various SP guns (see Artillery) and also for the so-called *Sturmpanzer IV* (*Brummbär* or Grizzly Bear), a massively armoured close-support assault gun

19. A cross between SP artillery and the true tank destroyer was the Ferdinand or Elefant with an 8·8cm L70 gun mounted on a tank chassis but with an improvised fighting room. This example, in Russia, has mottle green camouflage over yellow. (STT 4851)

with a 15cm howitzer (Fig. 22). Some 60 were built in 1944 mainly for the infantry gun companies of the Panzer Divisions. Other uses of the basic chassis were as Flakpanzer, munitions and bridge carriers and as carriers for the experimental '*Heuschrecke*' (Grasshopper) series of mobile artillery which never saw service in quantity.

Pzkpfw V AND VI (OLD STYLE): These were heavily armed designs stemming directly from the *Grosstraktor* experiments and produced only in prototype form during the mid-1930s. The Pzkw V had a turreted 7·5cm gun with a co-axial 3·7cm one, plus two MG 13s in another turret, while the Pzkw VI had the same chassis but with a 10·5cm weapon replacing the 7·5cm one! Neither was satisfactory, the chassis proving defective and the big crew – seven – uneconomic. The few built were used for propaganda purposes.

Pzkpfw V – LATER PANTHER (SD KFZ 171): The early Russian campaigns showed an urgent need for a better battle tank than the Type IV and in 1941 a competition was held between Daimler Benz and MAN for a tank in the 35 tonne range to take a 7·5cm L/70 gun concurrently under development by Rheinmetall Borsig. After close evaluation the MAN version was chosen, even though its weight had risen to 43 tonnes and very considerable teething problems were being encountered. As the Ausführung D it was produced from November 1942 but was put into service in Russia far too soon, with resultant serious setbacks. A modified version, oddly called Ausführung A, was produced in 1943–4 which overcame most of the difficulties and this was supplemented in

20. An excellent true Jagdpanzer, the Hetzer, consisted of a 7·5cm L48 gun in a well-sloped armoured hull. This example shows the close-defence machine gun and an odd camouflage pattern apparently of several dark colours over sand. (STT 7564)

1944 by the even more efficient Model G; this latter had redesigned hull armour and a modified suspension. (Pl. 15.)

This tank, officially designated 'Panther' by personal order of Hitler on February 22, 1944, was an excellent design: fast, well-armoured and ballistically well shaped, with the most effective 7·5cm gun in use during the war. In practice it was never entirely perfected and although a 'Panther II' was envisaged to mount the long 8·8cm gun in a Tiger-type turret, this never got beyond the prototype stage (it would have been Ausf. F). Some 6000 Panthers were built and the basic model was used also as a command vehicle, still with normal armament, and as an artillery observation tank (*Beobachtungspanther*), using up old D pattern chassis with a fixed 'turret' and mock main armament only; others were built as armoured recovery vehicles, with no armament but an open 'working compartment'. (*Bergepanther*) (Pl. 17).

JAGDPANTHER (SD KFZ 173): When it appeared that the basic tank might be overloaded by a turreted 8·8cm gun, a specialised jagdpanzer version was developed from late 1943 on. This, officially designated the *Jagdpanther* (Pl. 21) in February 1944, was a very neat adaptation which extended the hull sides and front upward into a fixed fighting compartment mounting the deadly 8·8cm L/71 gun in an anti-tank role. Some 230 of these were built, being allocated to Army units and not to Divisions. They were used almost entirely on the Russian front.

PZKW VI TIGER (SD KFZ 181): This originated from various pre-war experiments but was not finalised until May 1941 when a competition was held between Henschel and Porsche for a 45 tonne tank to carry the 8·8cm Kwk L/56, the tank version of the famous 8·8cm flak gun. Henschel won and their de-

21. Possibly the most efficient WW2 tank destroyer built in quantity:
    A Jagdpanther showing the neat way in which the standard Panther
    hull was continued up to form a well protected fighting
    compartment. (MH 7795)

sign, with a revised weight of no less than 56 tonnes, was put into production in August 1942 as the Tiger I (Ausf. E). Like the Panther it was rushed into service too early and the first models were often easily immobilised. It always had a tendency to unreliability from the strain that the sheer weight imposed on its components and the massive turret had a slow traverse for the same reason. Apart from these defects it was an extremely formidable opponent, its massive armour – up to 100mm thick – making it practically invulnerable except at short ranges and its excellent 8·8cm gun giving it almost unrivalled hitting power. Certainly its psychological value must have been almost as great as its material value to the German army since its virtues were wildly exaggerated by allied troops and it appears to have instilled far more terror than its size and numbers would warrant. (Pl. 10.)

The basic Ausführung E chassis was used also as a command tank; an armoured recovery vehicle which was really a towing vehicle consisting of a normal tank with gun removed and a winch fitted in the reversed turret; and a massive assault weapon comprising a 38cm rocket mortar in a fully armoured fighting compartment (*Sturmtiger*). Only a few of the latter were built, on chassis sent back for repair, and they were not very effective.

TIGER II (SD KFZ 182): From early 1944 on, the Tiger I was supplemented and, from August 1944 on, replaced in production by the Tiger II (Pl. 16). Once again the result of a Henschel/Porsche competition won by Henschel, this massive (67 tonne) tank was larger and mounted the 8·8cm Kwk L/71 in a much better shaped hull and turret; the first fifty actually had turrets produced

22. Products of the 1930s: A standard Panzerspähwagen (8-rad) Sd Kfz 231 leads one of its predecessors a Panzerspähwagen (6-rad) (Fu) Sd Kfz 233. Note that, with double steering, the cars are going in 'opposite' directions and that the rear car has a early-type frame aerial, a characteristic of German radio vehicles up to about 1942. In the background is a 1914–18 pattern horse-drawn field kitchen. (HU 3895)

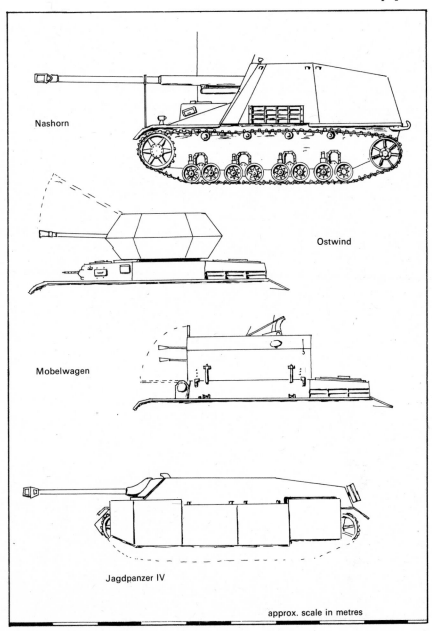

Nashorn

Ostwind

Mobelwagen

Jagdpanzer IV

approx. scale in metres

FIG 17 VARIATIONS on the PzIV

by Porsche in anticipation of a contract. It entered service in Russia in May 1944 and in the west in August; advanced in concept, it was yet underpowered and mechanically unreliable so that it never achieved its full potential. As with the other Tiger variants, the main problem was the great weight; if immobilised it was very difficult to tow away and many had to be abandoned for quite trivial reasons.

JAGDTIGER (SD KFZ 186): The final Tiger variant was the inevitable anti-tank/assault gun, known as the Jagdtiger and mounting a truly massive 12·8cm L/55 gun on a modified Tiger II chassis. At 76 tonnes it was the heaviest armoured vehicle to see service in World War II and its 250mm thick frontal armour made it virtually invulnerable to anti-tank fire. At the same time the normal Tiger weaknesses accentuated by the greater weight made it very unreliable and it was of little practical use except as a mobile pillbox. Only 48 were completed.

Light Armour

Armoured cars – *Panzerspähwagen*; armoured troop carriers (*Schutzenpanzerwagen* or SPW; Reconnaissance tanks – *Aufklarungspanzer*.

Light armour in the German army can be divided into two main categories, wheeled vehicles which were almost exclusively armoured cars but included some specialised command vehicles; and tracked or semi-tracked vehicles which included reconnaissance tanks, armoured cars and infantry carriers. Certain SP

23. The standard 4-wheeled scout car, in this case an **Sd Kfz 222**, with a multi-purpose gun mount. The 2cm cannon had been removed from this captured vehicle. (STT 2795)

guns could perhaps also be classed as light armour but are dealt with elsewhere. In general German light armour was influenced by the General Staff conception of its use for scouting and was designed to protect occupants from small arms fire only. All machines were therefore more lightly armoured than their allied equivalents but in general were also faster and more manoeuvrable.

WHEELED ARMOURED CARS

German armoured car development started as far back as 1926–7 with a fairly comprehensive specification for heavy armoured troop carrying vehicles. Among other things these had to have a road speed of 65kph and be able to: climb rock gradients of 1 in 3; cross 1·5metre wide trenches without stopping; wade one metre depth; weigh not more than 7·5 tonnes; be provided with double-steering front and rear so that a change of direction could be effected in 10 seconds without turning. An interesting requirement was that wheeltrack and tyres had to be such that, with tyres removed, the car could run on ordinary gauge railway lines using the inner wheel rims as flanges.

Magirus, Daimler Benz and Büssing started development of these machines in 'civilian' guise and they were the basis of all later heavy armoured cars. Meanwhile, in the early '30s, an interim type was urgently required. Fortunately – or perhaps inevitably – a civilian design of 1929 for a six-wheeled (four-wheel drive) lorry was suddenly found suitable for military work and the Daimler Benz chassis proved able to take an armoured superstructure. Although

24. Standard medium armoured personnel carrier: This Afrika Korps Sd Kfz 251/1 has a 3·7cm anti-tank gun replacing its forward machine gun; note the AA mounting for an MG34 at the rear. (MH 273)

not coming up to the original specification, the car could be equipped with double steering and went into service in 1933 with a modified body as the *Sd Kfz* 231 (*6-rad*) series. The series included cannon equipped scout cars with turrets and also special radio cars (*Funkwagen*) which had only a machine gun in a fixed shield surmounted by a huge frame antenna (Pl. 22). Some of the normal vehicles had more complicated communications equipment than usual and were designated *Panzerspähwagen* (*fu*).

This series was used operationally during the Polish and French campaigns but was then replaced by later eight-wheelers and withdrawn into a training role.

FOUR-WHEELED CARS (SD KFZ 221–3; 260–1): Chronologically the next vehicles to see service were the series of light scout cars that equipped many light armoured car companies of the Panzer Divisions for most of the war. These had their origin in the Einheits-programme heavy personnel carrier of 1935 which was fitted experimentally with a lightly armoured super-structure mounting either a machine gun (Kfz 13) or a wireless truck body (Kfz 14). These adaptations were not satisfactory, having only 8mm thick armour and an inadequate cross-country performance. They were, however, used in Poland and did provide experience for the 221 series. These were purpose-designed vehicles using the basic Einheits chassis but adapted to take a rear engine, all-wheel drive and double steering. A ballistically efficient body with sloping armour provided the following versions:

25. Specialist light armour, 1: The light armoured personnel carrier modified for the armoured car role as the Sd Kfz 250/9. (MH 3904)

Leichter Panzerspähwagen:
- (MG) Sd Kfz 221   1 × MG13 or MG34.
- mit 2·8cm PzB41. Sd Kfz 221   1 × 2·8cm A/T gun.
- (2cm) Sd Kfz 222   1 × 2cm cannon.
- (Fu) Sd Kfz 223   as 221.
Kleiner Panzerfunkwagen:
- Sd Kfz 260   nil.
- Sd Kfz 261   nil.

All armed vehicles had an open-topped turret and were powered by a V8 petrol engine giving a top speed of 80kph. Cross-country performance proved not entirely adequate, especially for Russia, and production was terminated in 1942 but they remained in service until the end of the war. The only real development was the provision from 1940–on of dual purpose (ground and AA) mountings for the 2cm cannon in some Kfz 222 vehicles (Pl. 23).

It was intended in 1941 to produce a new type using a shortened chassis and standard components from the then current eight-wheeled cars. Experimental versions were built with a 5cm gun and an MG42 in a revolving turret but although they were approved production never commenced. It is mentioned here because the turret was later used for the Puma eight-wheeled car (qv).

EIGHT-WHEELED CARS (8-RAD SD KFZ 231 SERIES AND SD KFZ 234 SERIES): Experimental work mentioned earlier led in 1934–5 to the development of an Einheits-programme standard eight-wheeled chassis with all-wheel drive, a rear-mounted V8 petrol engine, double-steering and ability to meet the 1926–7

26. Sd Kfz 251 as a self-propelled support gun for recce and Panzer Grenadier troops. (IWM)

specification. This chassis with various superstructures was adopted as the standard heavy reconnaissance vehicle and continued in that role until the end of the war, although production ceased in 1942. The following versions were built (Pl. 22):

Panzerspähwagen:
(8-rad Sd Kfz 231	2cm Kwk 38	
(8-rad) (Fu) Sd Kfz 232	2cm Kwk 38	
(8-rad) Sd Kfz 233	7·5cm StuK L/24	

Panzerfunkwagen:
(8-rad) Sd Kfz 263	nil

The 231 and 232 had revolving turrets, the 233 mounted its gun in an open-topped fighting compartment and the radio car was turretless. Note that because the definitive series took over the designations of the 6-wheeled cars, the clumsy prefix 8-rad was needed. Note too that this series did not mount either a 5cm or a long-barrelled 7·5cm gun. These vehicles were efficient armoured cars with a good cross-country performance and were taken out of production only because they were replaced with an even better vehicle the Sd Kfz 234.

The *Sd Kfz 234* series developed from a requirement in August 1940 for a heavy reconnaissance vehicle capable of operating in extremes of climate and with greater torsional rigidity. The result was a car having most of the characteristics of the 231 series but with a monocoque hull and a big Tatra 12-cylinder air-cooled diesel engine. With its excellent performance and its capability of mounting a wide range of weapons, this was undoubtedly one of

27. Sd Kfz 234 heavy armoured car PUMA, mounting the 5cm gun turret originally designed for a four-wheeled vehicle. (STT 7865)

the most advanced wheeled vehicles to be used by either side in the war; it gradually replaced the 231 series with the heavy armoured car companies from 1944 on.
The main variants were:

Schwerer Panzerspähwagen:
Sd Kfz 234/1   2cm KwK 38 + one MG
Sd Kfz 234/2 (Puma) 5cm KwK L/60 (Pl. 27)
Sd Kfz 234/3   7·5cm Kwk L/24
Sd Kfz 234/4   7·5cm KwK L/48

The 234/1 had an open turret, the 234/2 having the closed turret with 360 degree traverse already mentioned. Both the others had open-topped fighting compartments with only very limited traverse for the weapons; the 234/4 in particular is said to have been developed expressly at Hitler's order to provide a highly mobile, hard-hitting anti-tank weapon.

OTHER WHEELED VEHICLES: The only other wheeled light armour used in quantity were a number of Krupp-built 6-wheeled lorries that were fitted with armoured bodies as command vehicles, and two captured types. The first was the Austrian Wheel/tracked RR7 scout car which was impressed in small numbers as the *Sd Kfz 254*. This general design that could run either on wheels or on a retractable caterpillar track was a peculiarity of the Austrian army and was used in various forms by them; a machine gun carrier variant is shown in Pl. 11. The Sd Kfz 254 was used by the Germans mainly as an artillery observation vehicle.

The second foreign car was the French Panhard 38, about 150 of which were taken into service as the *Panzerspähwagen P204* (f). With a 2-cylinder petrol engine giving a top speed of 80kph on roads, and mounting a 2·5cm gun and a machine gun in a revolving turret, this was a reasonably effective vehicle. Like the German heavy cars it could be adapted to run on railway lines and some were so used as patrol vehicles from 1942 on.

TRACKED VEHICLES

The first fully-tracked light-armoured vehicles of the German army were adaptations of obsolete tank chassis. During the Polish campaign the cross-country limitations of the 'Einheits' series of wheeled troop carriers became obvious and, since purpose-built vehicles were still under development, a number of chassis – Pzkw I in particular – were converted into infantry carriers, possibly as ersatz for the little Kettenrad machine that was used later, (Pl. 3). A number of other tank chassis were also used later in small quantities for this purpose. The two major designs, however, were really light reconnaissance tanks and arose from the inadequacy of the Sd Kfz 221 series and, later of their half-track replacement. They were:

PANZERSPÄHWAGEN II (2CM KWK 38) (SD KFZ 123) LUCHS: This was a development in 1942 of the Pzkw II (so-called Neuer ausführung, with modified suspension (Fig. 16). It had improved suspension and overlapping road wheels. In prototype form as the VK1301, it came into service late in 1942 as the Pzkpfw II Ausf. L, a designation changed subsequently to that given above.

The first 100 had a 2cm gun and an MG 34 in a revolving turret, another 31 being built with a 5cm L/60 gun before production stopped in 1943.

SD KFZ 140: 70 of these vehicles were built from October 1943–on, combining the chassis of the Czech model 38 tank and the turret of the Sd Kfz 222, specifically for cross-country work in rugged terrain. The general characteristics were those of the Pzkw 38 (t) –qv.

HALF-TRACKED VEHICLES

The Blitzkrieg concept assumed that mobile infantry would be required to keep up with, and fight with, the tanks. Experiments in providing armoured carriers with cross-country performance started about 1935. A projected series of heavily gunned vehicles for the Light Divisions was not developed beyond the prototype stage, perhaps because of their complexity, but the 3-tonne half-track tractor chassis then being developed by Hanomag (Hannover Maschinenbau Gmbh) was chosen as the basis for a standard infantry carrier. It was to be capable of carrying a squad of 8–9 men, a driver and a commander; armour was to be capable of stopping small arms fire and the basic vehicle was to be equipped with mountings for machine guns and light anti-tank guns so that its crew could fight from it if required.

SD KFZ 251: The result was a series of vehicles first known as the *Mittlerer gepanzerter Mannschaftskraftwagen* and later as the *Mittlerer Schützenpanzerwagen* (SPW – medium armoured personnel carrier). The designations reflect the prevailing idea of using it as a carrying rather than as a fighting vehicle but it proved so useful that it was frequently employed in later years in the fighting role. Its crew dismounted only when necessary.

The basic vehicle consisted of what was really a three-quarter-track chassis, most of the vehicle weight being taken on the tracks while a pair of normally steered front wheels combined with track brakes served for steering. A wide variety of armoured superstructures for such diverse purposes as ambulance, munitions carrying, and close support artillery was mounted on this chassis with thin but well sloped armour. The vehicle had a good cross-country performance but was complicated to maintain and difficult to steer. (Pls. 6, 24, 26, 49).

The early series came into use in small numbers in 1939 and was used in Poland and the French campaign, but was not in full scale use until the 1941 Russian campaign. The early series of Ausführung A, B, and C were supplemented in 1943 by an improved and slightly modified Ausführung D and production was intensified so that all Panzer Divisions could be equipped with at least one SPW Abteilung in their infantry components. The basic vehicle was also used extensively by the infantry companies of the Recce abteilungen and by various Divisional services. The main variants were: (all prefixed Sd Kfz)

251/1	Troop carrier	251/12	Equipment carrier for survey troops
251/2	8·1cm mortar carrier		
251/3	Radio car	251/13	Artillery ranging and spotting vehicles
251/4	Towing vehicle for 7·5cm Infantry Gun	251/14	
		251/15	

251/5	Engineer vehicle	251/16	Flamethrower vehicle
251/6	Command Vehicle	251/17	2cm Flak
251/7	Engineer vehicle (equipment)	251/18	Artillery observation
251/8	Armoured ambulance	251/19	Telephone exchange
251/9	Close-support (7·5cm L/24)	251/20	Infra-red searchlight
251/10	Platoon Commander's		carrier
	vehicle (3·7cm PaK)	251/21	AA (triple-mounting)
251/11	Communications (telephone)	251/22	Anti-tank (7·5cm PaK 40)

Constant experimental work was undertaken to improve the design but no major alterations got past the prototype stage, mainly owing to production pressures. The basic inadequacies – complication, open-topped fighting compartment, underpowering of the chassis, particularly on 251/22 – were realised but demand was so great that the drop in production entailed by a new type could not be countenanced.

SD KFZ 250 SERIES (LEICHTER SPW): The Russian front in particular showed up the shortcomings of much reconnaissance equipment. It was decided to try to adapt the standard 1-tonne half-track chassis into an armoured carrier on the same lines as the Sd Kfz 251. The result was quite the most unsatisfactory German half-track of the war. Although superior to the Sd Kfz 221 series and to the normal four-wheeled trucks and motorcycle combinations, it was not as good as the big eight-wheeled armoured cars and was both heavy and underpowered. Nonetheless it was fairly widely used in a number of roles from 1942-on, running to twelve major variants and two versions with adapted bodies for munitions carrying and artillery observation. The basic vehicle could carry 4–5 men and was armed with one machine gun. An armoured car variant, the Sd Kfz 250/9 (Pl. 25), was hastily produced as 'ersatz' for the Sd Kfz 222 and mounting the same turret, but it never reached the prominence accorded it by allied Intelligence. The Sd Kfz 140/1 mentioned on p. 80, was intended as a replacement for this vehicle. Major variants were:

250/1	Basic infantry carrier	250/9	Arm'd Car (2cm KwK)
250/2	Telephone carrier	250/10	Platoon Commander
250/3	Radio car		(3·7cm PaK)
250/4	AA car	250/11	Light anti-tank
250/5	Observation Post		(2·8cm PzB41)
250/6	Ammunition carrier	250/12	Survey
250/7	8·1cm mortar carrier	252	Armoured munitions carrier
250/8	Close support (7·5cm L/24)	253	Observation post

Table 1 TYPICAL TANKS

	Pz Kpfw 1 Ausf B (Sd Kfz 101)	Pz Kpfw II D (Sd Kfz 121)	Pz Kpfw II F (Sd Kfz 121)	Pz Kpfw 38(t)	Pz Kpfw III E (Sd Kfz 141)	Pz Kpfw III J (Sd Kfz 141)	Pz Kpfw IV D (Sd Kfz 161)	Pz Kpfw IV H (Sd Kfz 161)	Pzkpfw Panther G (Sd Kfz 171)	Pz Kpfw Tiger E (Sd Kfz 181)	Pz Kpfw Tiger B (Sd Kfz 182)
Power											
Max. Range (km)	170	200	200	230	175	175	200	200	177	100	110
Max Speed (kph) Road/X-country	40*	55/19	40/19	42/15	40/18	40/19	40/20	38/16	46/24	38/20	38/17
H.P.	100	140	140	125	300	300	300	300	700	700	700
Engine	Maybach 6-cyl Water-Cooled	Maybach 6-cyl Water-Cooled	Maybach 6-cyl Water-Cooled	Praga 6-cyl Water-Cooled	Maybach 12-cyl Water-Cooled	Maybach 12-cyl Water-Cooled	Maybach 12-cyl Water-Cooled	Maybach 12-cyl Water-cooled	Maybach 12-cyl Water-Cooled	Maybach 12-cyl Water-Cooled	Maybach 12-cyl Water-Cooled
Armament											
Crew	2	3	3	4	5	5	5	5	5	5	5
Rounds for Main Weapon	1525	180	180	90	99	78	80	87	82	92	84
Subsidiary Weapons	—	1×7·92mm	1×7·92mm	1×7·92mm	1×7·92mm	2×7·92mm	2×7·92mm	2×7·92mm	3×7·92mm	2×7·92mm	3×7·92mm
Main Weapon	2×7·92mm MG13	2cm KwK 30 or 2cm KwK 38	2cm KwK 30 or 2cm KwK 38	3·7cm KwK A7 or L45	5cm KwK L42	5cm KwK L60	7·5cm KwK L24	7·5cm KwK L48	7·5cm KwK 42 L70	8·8cm KwK 36 L56	8·8cm KwK 43 L71
Dimensions											
Thickest Armour (mm)	13·0	30·0	35·0	25·0	30·0	50·0	30·0	80·0	80·0	100·0	150·0
Battle Weight (Tonnes)	6·00	10·00	9·50	9·73	19·50	22·30	20·00	25·00	44·80	55·00	69·70
Height (metres)	1·72	2·02	1·59	2·37	2·44	2·51	2·68	2·68	3·10	2·86	3·09
Width (metres)	2·06	2·30	2·28	2·06	2·91	2·95	2·86	3·29‡	3·43	3·73‡	3·75‡
Length over Hull (metres)	4·02	4·64	4·81	4·90	5·41	5·52	5·91	5·89	6·88	6·20	7·26
Length Over Gun Barrel (metres)	4·02	4·64	4·81	4·90	5·41	6·41	5·91	7·02	8·86	8·24	10·26

* Road speed   † Over skirt armour   ‡ In fighting trim

Table 2 STANDARD PURPOSE-BUILT ASSAULT GUNS

Vehicle	Length Over Gun Barrel (metres)	Length over Hull (metres)	Width (metres)	Height (metres)	Battle Weight (Tonnes)	Thickest Armour (mm)	Main Weapon	Subsidiary Weapons	Rounds for Main Weapon	Crew	Engine	H.P.	Max Speed (kph) Road/X-country	Max. Range (km)
Sturmgeschutz* III (Sd Kfz 142) — G	5·44	5·49	2·95	2·15	23·9	50·0	10·5cm StuH 42 L28	—	36	4	Maybach 12-cyl Water-cooled	300	40/24	169
(Sd Kfz 142/1) —		5·49	2·92	2·30	24·0	50·0	7·5cm StuK 40 L48	†	81	4	Maybach 12-cyl Water-cooled	300	40/24	169
Stu Pz Brummbär (Sd Kfz 166)	5·89	5·89	3·10‡	2·49	28·2	100·0	15cm StuH 43 L12	—†	38	5	Maybach 12-cyl Water-Cooled	300	40/?	210
Jgd Pz IV (Sd Kfz 162/1)	8·60 (L70)	6·02	3·18	1·85	24·0 to 25·8	80·0	7·5 StuK 42 (L70) or 7·5 Pak 39 L48	1×7·92mm	55	4	Maybach 12-cyl Water-Cooled	300	40/16	200
Jgd Pz Hetzer (Sd Kfz)	5·27	4·87	2·63	2·10	16·0	60·0	7·5cm Pak 39 L.48	1×7·92mm	40	4	Praga 6-cyl Water-Cooled	150	40/14	180
Jgd Pz Jagdpanther (Sd Kfz 173)	9·86	6·87	3·28	2·72	45·5	80·0	8·8cm Pak 43/3 L/71	1×7·92mm	60	5	Maybach 12-cyl Water-Cooled	700	40/24	210
Jgd Pz Jagdtiger‡ (Sd Kfz 186)	10·66	7·80	3·63	2·82	71·1	150·0	12·8 Pak 44 L55	1×7·92mm	38	6	Maybach 12-cyl Water-Cooled	700	38/17	170
Jgd Pz Elefant (Sd Kfz 184s)	8·14	6·80	3·43	2·97	68	200·0	8·8cm Pak 43/2 L71	—†	50	6	Maybach 12-cyl Water-Cooled (coupled)	2×320	20/?	150

* Also models with other 7·5-cm guns

† Some had 1×7·92mm MG

‡Some slight variations

Table 3 LIGHT ARMOUR

Vehicle	Max. Range (km)	Max Speed (kph) Road/X-country	H.P.	Engine	Crew	Rounds for Main Weapon	Subsidiary Weapons	Main Weapon	Thickest Armour (mm)	Battle Weight (Tonnes)	Height (metres)	Width (metres)	Length Over Gun Barrel (metres)
Sd Kfz 231 (6 rad)	250	60	65	Bussing 4-cyl Water-Cooled	4	200	—	2cm KwK 30	14·5	5·00	2·24	1·85	5·61
Sd Kfz 222	320	80	75	Horch 4-cyl Water-Cooled	3	180	1×7·92mm	2cm KwK 30 or 2cm KwK 38	14·5	4·80	2·06	2·00	4·72
Sd Kfz 231 (8 rad)	300	85	150	Bussing 8-cyl Water-Cooled	4	180	—	2cm KwK 30 or 2cm KWK 38	14·5	8·20	2·34	2·21	5·80
Sd Kfz 234	600	85	220	Tatra 12-cyl Diesel Air-Cooled	4	280 / 55	1×7·92mm / —	2cm KwK 38 or 5cm KwK 39/1 L60 or 7·5cm KwK L24 or 7·5cm PaK 40	30·0	10·50 to 11·00	2·10 to 2·29	2·36	6·02
Sd Kfz 123 'Luchs'	250	60	180	Maybach 6-cyl Water-Cooled	4	330 / 180	1×7·92mm	2cm KwK 38 or 5cm KwK 39/1	30·0.	11·80	2·13	2·49	4·63
Pz Spw P204(f)	350	80	115	Panhard 4-cyl Water-Cooled	4	150	1×7·5mm	2·5cm KwK (f)	20·0	8·20	2·37	2·00	4·60
le SPW Sd Kfz 250	320	60	100	Maybach 6-cyl Water-cooled	up to 6	—	see p. 81	Various see p. 81	12·0	5·70	1·66*	1·95	4·56
m SPW Sd Kfz 251	300	50	120	Maybach 6-cyl Water-Cooled	up to12	—	see p. 80	Various see p. 80	12·0	8·50	1·75*	2·10	5·80

Column groups: *Power* — Max. Range, Max Speed, H.P., Engine. *Armament* — Crew, Rounds for Main Weapon, Subsidiary Weapons, Main Weapon. *Dimensions* — Thickest Armour, Battle Weight, Height, Width, Length Over Gun Barrel.

* Top of armour, basic version

Motor Transport

When the German army was reformed in the early 1930s, it was built up by professionals who insisted that the 'Blitzkrieg' concept required the right vehicles for each job. Initially the motorisation of the army was achieved by building special bodies on various commercial car and light lorry chassis, these being designated Pkw (o) – Personnel carriers: commercially available chassis – and Lkw (o) – load carriers, ditto. Widely seen and admired in the very effective propaganda photographs of the time, these were not in practice very efficient for fighting since the cars were in general 4 × 2 (wheels/drive) vehicles with a low ground clearance and little cross-country capability. The lorries were usually 6 × 4 vehicles dating from the late 1920s in concept, although military uses had, it would appear, been borne in mind during their design. Perhaps the most efficient was the Krupp LH243 'boxer' – so-called from its horizontally-opposed engine (Pl. 49, Fig. 19) – that was used in large numbers in various roles.

In the mid-1930s, therefore, design and production was initiated of a whole series of specialised infantry carriers and load-carrying vehicles known as the *Einheits* (standard) series. Initially these were all-wheeled, being based on sophisticated 4 × 2, 4 × 4 and 6 × 4 chassis with various patterns of body-work. They were intended mainly as cross-country vehicles (*Geländegangig*) and at the same time heavy motorcycle combinations were widely adopted as the standard mounts for recce units.

From 1935 on, the army also developed a standardised and very successful series of semi-tracked vehicles, mainly as load carriers and prime movers but

28. Standard 1-tonne half-track vehicles towing 5cm PAK 38 guns.
   (MH 183)

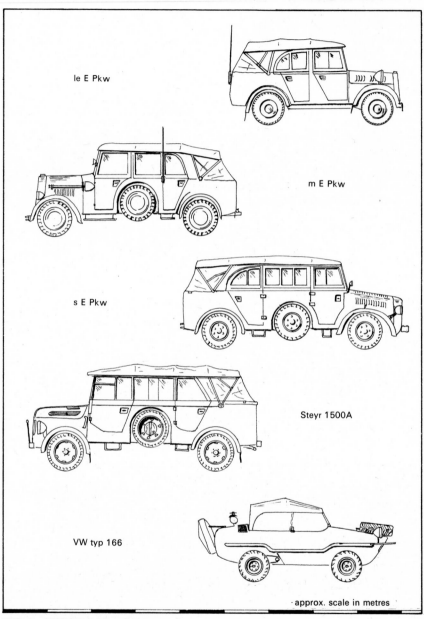

le E Pkw

m E Pkw

s E Pkw

Steyr 1500A

VW typ 166

approx. scale in metres

FIG 18 STANDARD CARS

including armoured personnel carriers at a later date (see p. 80). The complete series included vehicles of 1 tonne, 3t, 5t, 8t, 12t, and 18t rated haulage capacity, many being later adapted as self-propelled gun mountings. All were equipped with needle-roller bearings and torsion-bar suspension on the track units, rubber track pads, heavy-duty overlapping bogie wheels and 'Cletrac' type geared track steering for cross-country work; this enabled them also to slew round extremely quickly on hard surfaces. These vehicles were continually developed and served with all arms right up to the end of the war. Except for the American M3 series the allies never had true equivalents and over 25,000 in all were produced. In general the 1-tonnes were used as light artillery tractors (Pl. 28); 2cm gun mounts and as special purpose vehicles (eg decontamination); the 3-tonne series were lorries and artillery prime movers for the 10·5cm field guns and 7·5cm anti-tank guns (Pl. 29); 5 and 8 tonnes were produced mainly as artillery tractors with cross-bench seating (Pl. 7) and as SP AA guns – the 8 tonne series being the standard tractor for the 8·8cm and the medium artillery; the 12 tonnes, also with passenger seating, were used for medium and heavy artillery, while the 18 tonnes were mainly built with truck bodies and fitted with winches for vehicle and tank retrieval. For the latter operation they were often coupled in tandem.

The 'standard' vehicle programme, however, ran into considerable difficulties owing to the complications both of production and maintenance of such sophisticated designs; the mittlerer (medium) Ekw chassis for example had over 100 greasing points alone. In the outcome only four chassis were continued in production during the war and two of these were discontinued quite early on. The first was the light lorry (le E Lkw) produced from 1937–40 (Fig. 19). This was a 6×6 chassis capable of carrying $2\frac{1}{2}$ tonnes and powered by a six-cylinder diesel engine driving through a four-speed box with auxiliary

29. Standard 3-tonne half-track prime mover with truck body, towing an leFH18. (PC 370)

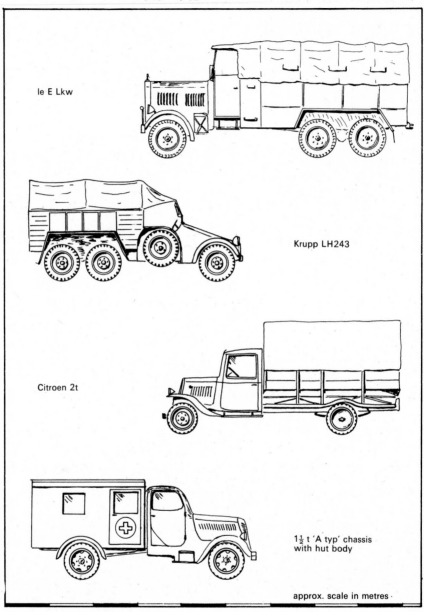

le E Lkw

Krupp LH243

Citroen 2t

$1\frac{1}{2}$ t 'A typ' chassis
with hut body

approx. scale in metres ·

FIG 19 TYPICAL LIGHTLORRIES

gearing for cross-country work. The other three were the light, medium and heavy car chassis (Fig. 18) all with the following features:

(i) permanent four-wheel drive with a torque distributor and with independent suspension on all wheels.

(ii) a self-locking rear differential – fitted also to the front axle of the le E Pkw.

(iii) a very low auxiliary gear for cross-country work.

Early models also had stub axles amidships to carry the spare wheels and had four-wheel steering but these features were soon discontinued. In practice the light car (Pl. 30) was quickly replaced by the Volkswagen (Pl. 31), the medium one went out of production in 1943 when the heavy car was also replaced by a new Steyr design.

It was therefore obvious that the Einheits programme would never meet the numerical needs of even the elite Divisions and in 1938 Colonel (later General) von Schell reorganised military production in the so-called Schell Programme. This persuaded the Wehrmacht to reduce its standard vehicles to the four mentioned above and to accept as replacement a limited number of modified commercial types; in all it reduced the wide variety of models in military and civil production from 113 to 30 (trucks); 52 to 19 (cars); and 150 to 30 (motorcycles) so that in case of need the army would be able to commandeer civilian vehicles without drastically complicating the spares situation. Load classes were standardised at $1\frac{1}{2}$, 3 and $4\frac{1}{2}$ tonnes, and two variants of each chassis type were authorised, the S-Typ (standard) 4 × 2 pattern mainly for civilian use; and the A-Typ (*Allradantrieb*), 4 × 4 military version. Successful designs were often produced by several firms the most well-known being the Opel

30. Einheits-programme light car, showing typical square bodywork and high ground clearance. This is a captured example with British markings. (STT 6994)

'Blitz' 3-tonne also built widely by Ford (Pl. 32) and the $4\frac{1}{2}$ tonne Büssing and Mercedes Benz designs.

The opening years of the war, and especially the Russian campaigns, showed up two weaknesses in German motor transport: the specialised Einheits vehicles were too complicated for reliability in rugged conditions, while Schell-Programme vehicles did not always have the performance needed; and even with the Schell simplifications there were in any case not enough vehicles to cope with the rapidly expanding need. This last problem was never entirely solved even though all resources of occupied countries were utilised.

The first weakness gave rise to a number of improvisations and a few new 'standard' vehicles. Most important of the improvisations was the so-called *Maultier*, or Mule family of half-track hybrid lorries. Reputedly initiated in the field by Waffen SS units who replaced the rear wheels of $4\frac{1}{2}$ tonne vehicles with a tracked unit based on Pzkw I and II components (Pl. 33), these were intended to achieve better cross-country performance in mud and snow. They were so successful that quantity production of modified versions on both 3 and $4\frac{1}{2}$ tonne chassis was undertaken. Load class was reduced because of increased suspension weight, Opel and Klockner producing 2-tonnes and Mercedes a 4-tonne.

The major standard vehicles introduced during the war were five in number. First and by far the most numerous was the famous Volkswagen Typ 82 *Kubelwagen* (Pl. 31), developed from the pre-war 'Peoples Car'. A simple 4×2 chassis with air-cooled engine and rugged bodywork this was at first regarded rather dubiously but test examples sent to the Russian front proved so successful that mass production commenced very quickly. An amphibious

31. The standard car for most of the war: Volkswagen Type 82 Kübelwagen. (STT 9792)

32. Typical Schell Programme 3-tonne, an Opel Blitz here seen with British markings and a 'civilian' pattern cab. (STT 6985)

variant, the VW166 *Schwimmwagen* with optional 4-wheel drive and a low auxiliary gear (Fig. 18) proved even more useful and replaced the motorcycles in many armoured reconnaissance units from 1942. It was, however, more specialised than the Typ 82 and production ceased in 1944 when the tactical situation changed.

The next most useful vehicle was the Steyr 1500A, again a private venture design, which replaced the heavy car from 1943–on. This was a big $1\frac{1}{2}$ tonne load carrier, also produced in car form (Fig. 18), with a V8 air-cooled engine and optional four-wheel drive, plus the usual auxiliary gearbox for cross-country work. Relatively simple, it proved popular on all fronts, especially in Russia where rugged simplicity and air-cooled engines were most suited to the extreme climatic conditions! The other standard designs built in quantity were three lorries, also benefitting from the experience of war. Two were attempts to provide simplified transport with the capabilities of the standard half-tracks. They were the *Schwerer Wehrmachtsschlepper* (heavy tractor, or SWS) a 5-tonne which replaced the 5-tonne half-track in production from 1944 on, and the *Raupenschlepper Ost* (tracked tractor, East). The SWS was a conventional half-track chassis but without most of the sophisticated design features of the standard range. It was produced mainly as a lorry although experiments were made both with fully armoured versions, in particular as mounts for rocket projectors, and with armoured-cab versions to mount various light guns. The Raupenschlepper Ost (RSO) in service from 1944, was the result of a competition to provide a crude but efficient prime mover for use by the infantry Divisions in Russia. It was a small fully tracked lorry (Pl. 35) showing Russian influence in its design, and could pull loads up to the 10·5cm gun-howitzer. Some chassis were used as SP gun mounts. Its competitor, the *Radschlepper Ost* (wheeled tractor, East) was an odd vehicle with huge cleated wheels which proved susceptible to vibration. Only 200 were built before it was dropped in favour of the RSO. The third lorry was a Czech design from the firm of Tatra and was a 6 × 6, 6½ tonne. Once again this had an air-cooled engine, in this case a V12 diesel, and was adopted as a standard type from 1943 on, especially for supply work. It was the only standard type with a capacity greater than 4½ tonnes.

Even with these simplified designs, however, there were never more than enough standard vehicles barely to equip the elite divisions. Other units and the huge number of supply columns of various types had to rely on a fantastic variety of impressed civilian types and captured enemy ones. Considerable efforts were made to keep this variety to a minimum. Production capacity in the Reich and in occupied territories was integrated as far as possible: Germany, Czechoslovakia and Austria produced standard equipment as did Ford in the Netherlands and certain French works; Italy undertook little production even after her collapse in 1943, but did provide a useful windfall of existing equipment. Otherwise, reasonably efficient equipment in production when a country was occupied was continued with. Thus for example, the German army took on charge during the war almost 6000 of the 'standard' Citroen 2-tonne, 4 × 2 truck (Fig. 19).

Even so it was necessary to press into service almost anything that had wheels and an engine, and by 1942 the spares and maintenance situation was so bad that the '*Sperrtypen*' or prohibited vehicles order had to be enacted. This meant that where less than a certain number of one type – originally 150 – was in

33. 4½–tonne Bussing-Nag lorry converted to a Maultier by use of PzII suspension components. This example has the wood-and-pressed cardboard 'Einheitsfahrerhaus' or standard cab. (IWM)

service, attempts were made to concentrate them and down grade them to rear-echelon service only; those held by forward units were sent back for cannibalisation when beyond immediate repair.

Production repair and use of what vehicles were available were not made easier by increasing shortages of steel and fuel. It was not possible to do much to reduce the use of steel although a pressed-cardboard and wood cab known as the *Einheitsfahrerhaus* (standard driver's cab, Pl. 33) often replaced the usual pressed steel ones in later years. Fairly widespread use was, however, made of producer-gas installations to provide fuel in place of petrol. These, in particular the Imbert wood-burning pattern, were used both in rear formations and, later in second line and training units. They were quite successful, up to 80 per cent of rated power being available from modified engines, although this had the disadvantage that they could not be quickly reconverted to petrol. The unit was, however, both bulky and inconvenient to use.

To sum up, the German front line tactical transport was generally of high quality and often superior to allied equivalents. There was, however, never nearly enough to go round and even for the motorised units reliance had to be placed on a wide variety of impressed, captured or modified civilian vehicles scraped together from all over the place; one motorised division in France in 1944 is recorded as having no less than 70 distinct types on its inventory.

34. The Kettenkrad or motor cycle tractor, here in British hands but with markings of 3rd Motorcycle Coy, 15 Pz Division. Note earlier tactical markings at rear, partly obliterated. (IWM)

Table 4 TYPICAL STANDARD M.T.

Basic Vehicle	Wheels/ Drive	Length (m)	Width (m)	Height (m)	Engine Cyls/Cooling (W or A)/CC	H.P.	Weight (kg)
CARS le E. Pkw (Kfz 2)	4×4	3·85	1·69	1·90	4/W/1997	50	1700
m E Pkw (Kfz 15)	4×4	4·74	1·85	2·05*	6–8/W/2983*	68 or 80	2500
S. E. Pkw (Kfz 69)	4×4	4·85	2·00	2·04	V8/W/3823	81	3150
VW Typ 82 (Kfz 1)	4×2	3·74	1·60	1·65	4/A/985*	24	685
VW Typ 166 (Kfz 1/20)	4×4	3·83	1·48	1·62	4/A/1131	25	910
Steyr 1500A (Kfz 21)	4×4	5·08	1·85	2·10	V8/A/3517	85	3630
LORRIES Le E Lkw (2t)	6×4	5·85	2·26	2·60	6/W/	85	4900
Opel Btitz (3t)	4×2(S) 4×4(A)	6·02	2·27	2·18	6/W/3610	74	2810
Bussing (4¼t)	4×4	8·16	2·35	3·10	6/W/	105	5900
Tatra (6½t)	6×6	8·55	2·50	3·10	V12/A/14825	210	8350
Raupenschlepper Ost. (1½t)	T	4·425	1·99*	2·53	V8/A/3517	85	3500
Maultier on Opel 3t chassis	T	6·00	2·28	2·71	6/W/3626	68	3930
STD HALF-TRACKS Kettenrad (Sd kfz 22)	T	3·00	1·00	1·20	4/W/1478	36	1235
1-tonner (Sd Kfz 10)	T	4·75	1·84	1·62	6/W/	100	3400
3-tonner (Sd Kfz 11)	T	5·50	2·00	2·20	6/W/	100	5550
5-tonner (Sd Kfz 6)	T	6·33	2·26	2·27	6/W/	100	7500
SWS (5t)	T	6·68	2·50	2·83	6/W/	100	9500
8-tonner (Sd Kfz 7)	T	6·85	2·40	2·76	6/W/	140	9750
12-tonner (Sd Kfz 28)	T	7·10	2·50	2·80	V12/W/	185	13100
18-tonner (Sd Kfz 9)	T	8·33	2·60	2·85	V12/W/	230	15470

* Minor variations in series depending on manufacturer.

Horse-drawn Transport

German Divisional horse-drawn transport was designed to be as efficient as such vehicles could be. It was issued both to Infantry Divisions and to infantry corps supply columns on a definite scale and can be divided into two major types: battle transport (*Gefechtstross*) and support or supply transport.

The battle transport, issued to infantry formations down to platoon level, was intended for carriage of ready-to-use supplies and heavy weapons. The intended vehicles were modern, light and often steel-bodied. Mounted on pneumatic tyres, they comprised two-horse wagons (usually the Hf 7 or *Stahlfeldwagen* – Steel fieldcart – and various patterns of one and two-horse limber and trailer units. The most common were the If 8 *Infanteriekarren*, small load carriers with tarpaulin covers and capable of taking an AA machine gun mounting; and the two-horse MG Wagen 36 (Fig. 20) with its communications variants. These were true limbers carrying 2–3 men and coupled to two-wheeled caissons containing guns, tripods and ammunition, or other equipment; they were issued to the heavy-machine gun sections using MG 34s and MG 42s (see Ch. 6). Typical allocations to a 1944 pattern infantry rifle company were: HQ one If8; each rifle Zug two If8; heavy machine gun Staffel one Hf7 and two If8.

The support vehicles were often of more archaic pattern dating back in some cases to WWI and included the very widely used Hf1 light field cart, a wooden vehicle pulled by two horses (Pl. 36) and various limber and trailer combinations

35. The Raupenschlepper Ost, a light tracked vehicle built in quantity especially for the Russian front. (PC 408)

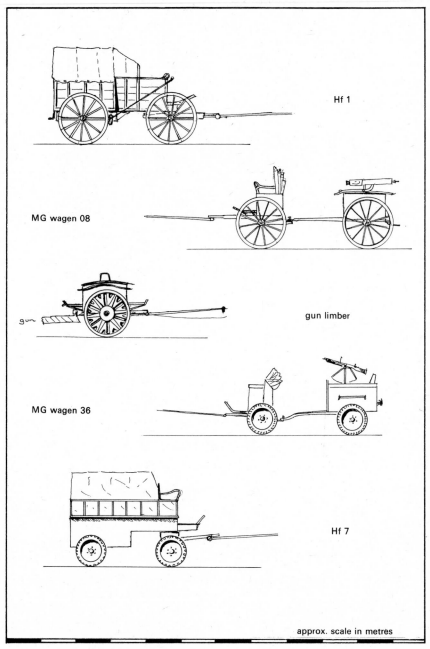

Hf 1

MG wagen 08

gun limber

MG wagen 36

Hf 7

approx. scale in metres

FIG 20 HORSE DRAWN VEHICLES

36. A common sight: Light field wagons (IF 1) being towed behind a
prime mover. Note, unusually, the unit insignia on the rear one
showing they belong to an artillery regiment.   (MH 9416)

37. Combat engineer troops with light bridging equipment
(Bruckengerat K) mounted on Sd Kfz 251/5s.   (STT 6996)

both as weapons carriers and as communications vehicles. Four-horse carts were used by support companies which also contained similar water tank wagons, field kitchens etc (a field kitchen can be seen in Pl. 22). Typical examples of vehicles are shown in Fig. 20, but civilian vehicles were often commandeered also.

Artillery vehicles included four- and six-horse limbers; an example is shown in Fig. 20 and Pl. 38 shows a horse-drawn 10·5cm haubitze.

Artillery

The German artillery used during WW2 was a curious mixture of very uninspired and very advanced designs. Anti-tank weapons, which started on a par with other countries' guns, developed rapidly and very successfully under the stress of war conditions, as did guns for special circumstances (eg airborne use; multi-barrelled mortars). On the other hand field and medium equipments developed only in so far as the basic pre-war designs could be upgraded by improvements to their ballistic performance and carriages. The main lines of development were:

- a) increase in barrel length for a specified calibre, with parallel development of the propellant; this gave greater muzzle-velocity and accuracy.
- b) reduction in projectile weight to achieve the same effect (see note on projectiles).
- c) rocket assistance – used operationally especially with medium equipments but found to decrease accuracy.

38. Light anti-tank weapons 1: The original 3·7cm gun was upgraded by equipping it to fire anti-tank grenades. This otherwise standard gun on its normal carriage has an anti-tank grenade (Panzergranate 40) in position.   (MH 297)

39. Its successor as a light infantry-operated weapon was the
Schwerepanzerbuchse 2·8cm coned bore equipment, here in its
airborne guise with small wheels and lightened carriage. (NA 4751)

Particular attention was paid to using normal artillery for the anti-tank role
hollow charge projectiles being used by all low and medium velocity equipments,
and great ingenuity was shown in making artillery more mobile by providing it
with self-propelled chassis; the original assault guns were ahead of all other
countries in their concept and development.

It is worth noting here that the Germans used four major designations for
their artillery besides the overall term 'Geschutz' which simply means gun.
These were *Kanone* – equivalent to the allied 'gun' and indicating a high-
muzzle velocity, flat trajectory weapon; *Haubitze*, equivalent to the allied
gun-howitzer which could fire in both the upper and lower registers; *Mörser*,
or howitzer, that fired in the upper register only, lobbing its shells; and *Werfer*
or mortar. It may also be worth noting that there were two basic patterns of
carriage – the box-trail, which was composed of girders rigidly braced together,
and the split trail which had movable 'legs' splayed out for firing.

INTRODUCTORY NOTE ON PROJECTILES

Besides the normal smoke, high explosive (HE) and solid, armour piercing
shells (AP), the Germans used a number of special shot. These were designed
specifically to increase the power of both conventional artillery and purpose-
designed anti-tank artillery in the anti-armour role. They were all designed to
increase speed – since penetration of armour normally depended on velocity of
the shot – or to compensate for the lower muzzle velocities of gun-howitzers
and similar pieces. They were:

SKIRTED SHOT: This pattern of shot was designed for use in the so-called coned-bore guns to provide increased muzzle velocity for a given calibre. The barrel was wider in diameter at the breech than at the muzzle and the shot had collapsible skirts at its base and shoulder. These ensured, respectively, increased base area for the propellant charge to act on and correct centering of the shot in the barrel. The 'skirts' were squeezed into annular recesses on the shot as it progressed down the barrel.

SABOT: This was a solid shell of smaller diameter than the gun barrel. It was encased in light, outer rings which fitted the barrel and fell away as the shot left the gun. The purpose was to allow large calibre artillery to fire armour piercing projectiles at an enhanced muzzle velocity.

COMPOSITE RIGID: This was, in effect, a non-discarding sabot, the solid core being surrounded by a lightweight casing which would break away on impact with the target.

HOLLOW CHARGE: This was a projectile designed to allow artillery pieces with low muzzle velocities to be used in an anti-tank role. It was filled with a potent incendiary charge which ignited on contact and was so shaped that it burned its way through the armour with a 'jet of flame' in advance of its solid rear section. Anti-tank rocket projectors and Panzerfausts worked on this principle also (see p. 141).

ANTI-TANK ARTILLERY: (*Panzerabwehrkanonen*, or Pak)

In the German army, tank guns (Kampfwagenkanone – KwK), assault gun weapons (StuK) and anti-tank guns (PaK) developed along parallel lines, any particular tank weapon usually having its assault and anti-tank equivalents. For their period, the German high velocity guns were among the most advanced

40. Close support was provided by infantry guns. These are sIG 33 15cm guns in standard form. (STT 7701)

41. Another method was the light nebelwerfer or multi-barrelled mortar. This damaged example is a 6-barrelled, towed version that normally travelled on a two-wheeled carriage. (WJKD)

anywhere, being in general considerably superior to their direct western allied equivalents and at least equal to their Russian counterparts. A particular advantage was that, while British and American anti-tank equipments were mostly designed to fire only solid shot, the Germans, like the Russians, always regarded their guns as dual purpose and designed them for both AP and HE projectiles.

At the beginning of the war, the standard German anti-tank equipment was the 3·7cm Pak 35/36 dating from about 1934 and used both as a towed weapon and mounted on SP chassis. Although all planning was based on this model – for example the original casemates of the Siegfried Line could take nothing bigger – it soon proved embarrassingly inadequate against modern armour and urgent measures had to be taken to remedy the situation. An interim solution was the provision of *Panzergranate 40* (anti-tank grenade 40) hollow charge projectiles (Pl. 38) and the introduction into service in limited numbers of both indigenous and captured makeshift equipments.

The indigenous gun was the so-called *4·2cm le Pak 41*, a coned bore weapon with a muzzle diameter of 2·8cm and mounted on a modified 3·7cm carriage; it was designed for a two man crew. The captured equipments were the old French 7·5cm field gun mounted on a Pak 35 chassis as the 7·5cm *Pak 39*; and the Czech 4·7cm gun which was used mainly on SP chassis as a mobile weapon.

Meanwhile development had been taking place of the first really effective anti-tank equipment used by either side. This, which came into service at the end of 1940, was the long-barrel *5cm Pak 38* (Pl. 28). It was a towed weapon, having a muzzle brake, a double shield and a well-designed split trail carriage

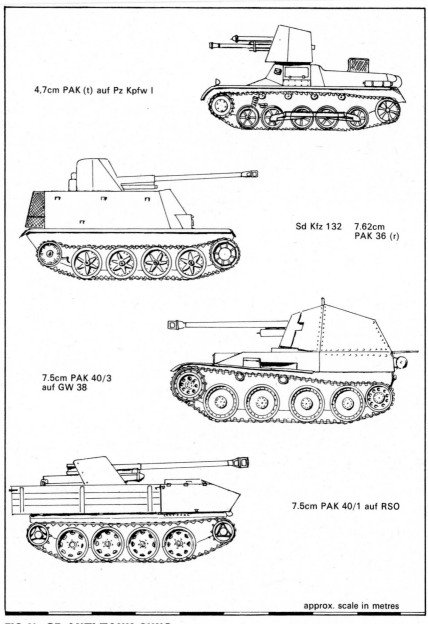

4,7cm PAK (t) auf Pz Kpfw I

Sd Kfz 132   7.62cm
PAK 36 (r)

7.5cm PAK 40/3
auf GW 38

7.5cm PAK 40/1 auf RSO

approx. scale in metres

FIG 21   SP ANTI-TANK GUNS

with torsion bar suspension – a feature of all succeeding equipments which made for mobility, lightness and a low silhouette. An excellent weapon by 1941 standards, it was never entirely replaced and its tank gun derivative the 5cm KwK L60 also served in various forms until the end of the war.

By the end of 1941, however, the Russian campaign had showed that all existing equipments were inadequate when matched against the T34 tanks and rapid action again had to be taken. To start with, a number of the excellent Russian 7·62cm field guns, captured in the first big attacks, were modified for use both as towed and self-propelled anti-tank weapons. At the same time, development was started of two competing purpose-designed guns of 7·5cm calibre to replace the 5cm gun in the heavy anti-tank role and of a very light weapon to replace the 3·7cm gun for infantry use.

The light weapon was the *2·8cm SPBZ41*. Commonly known as the 20/28 gun, this was actually classed as a heavy anti-tank rifle (*Schwere Panzerbuchse*) and was a coned bore equipment reducing to 20mm calibre at the muzzle. Allied intelligence sources are unanimous in noting this gun as a retrograde step so far as calibre is concerned but this is only partly true. It was an excellent light anti-vehicle weapon, simple to fire, manageable by one man and a loader, and mounted on a light two-wheeled carriage that enabled it to be effectively used even by marching infantry units. An even lighter version for airborne use, with small wheels and no shield was also produced under the same designation and this weighed only 206lb in all. (Pl. 39.)

The heavy weapons were the *7·5cm Pak 40*, designed by Rheinmetall Borsig, which became the standard Divisional anti-tank gun; and the *7·5cm Pak 41* a coned-bore equipment designed by Krupp in direct competition. This

42. Field artillery: a standard late-model 10·5cm gun-howitzer leFH 18/40. This example shows clearly the split-trail carriage and muzzle brake with baffles. (WJKD)

latter weapon was lighter and had an outstanding performance up to 1000m but its effectiveness fell off sharply thereafter and it was complicated to produce. As a result only 150 were built.

The *7·5cm Pak 40* (Pl. 47), however, was a simple, excellent weapon capable of destroying contemporary armour at ranges of over 1500m and still good enough to account for any British or American tank right up to the war's end. Its main disadvantage was a high overall weight which reduced manoeuvre-ability when towed, although its sloped shield and low silhouette gave useful protection to the crew. It was used also as the basis for various SP equipments, in at least two cases being mounted complete except for its wheels. The KwK equivalent, the 7·5cm KwK L/48 and its derivative the 7·5cm KwK L/70, were used more often in specialist hunter vehicles.

By late 1942, however, heavy Russian tanks were taxing the capabilities even of the 7·5cm gun and it was decided to modify the current 8·8cm anti-aircraft (Flak) gun for an anti-tank role. The originals had been used effectively in a ground role by Rommel in Africa and the basic weapon, the 8·8cm Flak 41 and 43 was without doubt the finest gun then in existence. It suffered from a very high silhouette, inadequate crew shielding and the need partly to dis-assemble its cruciform carriage before firing. The modification, which was known as the *8·8cm Pak 43*, and came into service in that year, had a very low silhouette with a well-sloped shield. It was still on a cruciform carriage but could be brought into action simply by lowering jacks and had a semi-automatic fire-control system. As a dual purpose weapon it equipped GHQ units, army

43. Field artillery 2: sFH 18 series medium gun howitzers. The 'travelling' and 'firing' position for the recoil spades or anchors can be seen on the two nearest guns. Note camouflage finish. (STT 5605)

flak units (Heeresflak) and some Divisional AA abteilungen. It was capable of knocking out any allied tank at ranges of up to 2000m and it was also a highly lethal anti-infantry weapon firing fused shell to produce air-bursts.

The complex cruciform carriage of the weapon, however, was in short supply and so the basic gun was also mounted on a two-wheeled field carriage as the *8·8cm Pak 43/41*. This was a compromise to achieve quick production, having a carriage made up from elements of that of the 10·5cm gun-howitzer le FH 18/40 (qv) matched with wheels from the s18, 15cm series of guns. Ballistic performance was unaltered as it was in the various SP mountings described at the end of this section.

These two guns formed the backbone of the heavy anti-tank units until the end of the war, although by 1945 an even heavier weapon had been developed. This was the *12·8cm PaK*, an outstanding equipment which fortunately was not produced in quantity. It had a very low silhouette, an efficient cruciform chassis from which it could be fired without dismantling and an armour penetration of 200mm at 30 degrees, at a range of 1000m. Fire-control was semi-automatic.

All major anti-tank equipments were at one time or another mounted on SP chassis as *Panzerjaeger* (tank hunters) and some were also mounted in the specialised *Jagdpanzer* (hunter tanks) which had purpose-designed hulls. The panzerjaeger mountings varied from small numbers of experimental vehicles (eg 3·7cm gun on the British Bren Carrier; 7·62cm gun on heavy half-track – DIANA) to large scale production runs as typified by the *Marder* (Marten)

44. SP artillery 1: The *Wespe*, a Pz II chassis mounting a 10·5cm field gun-howitzer, in this case an leFH18M. Note the battery letter, the cross, and the green or earth streaks over yellow finish. (STT 7233)

I, II, and III series. Typical examples are shown in Fig. 21 and a list of the main ones is given below.

3·7cm: Sd Kfz 251;

2·8cm: Sd Kfz 250; Sd Kfz 222.

5cm: PUMA

7·5cm: Marder II (PzII); Marder III (Pz 38 (t)); Sd Kfz 251/22;
          Sd Kfz 234/4; Raupenschlepper Ost; PzIII Sturmgeschütz

7·62cm: Pz II Ausf D (Sd Kfz 132); Pz 38t (Sd Kfz 139)

8·8cm: Nashorn (Rhinoscerous) on Typ III/IV (Fig. 17); Elefant (on
          Porsche Tiger) (Pl. 19)

By and large these adaptations either mounted the gun complete or added an open-topped or covered fighting room. They were not true battle-armour and the one attempt to use Elefants in this fashion ended disastrously.

45. Medium SP artillery: HUMMEL, consisting of an sFH18 gun-howitzer on a hybrid Type III/IV chassis. The netting camouflage is quite typical of guns operating in fairly open country. (MH 374)

Table 5 ANTI-TANK ARTILLERY

Piece	Calibre/ length ratio	In Travelling Order Length (metres)	Width (metres)	Height (metres)	Battle weight (kg)	Rate of fire (r.p.m.)	(m/s) muzzle velocity	L of Penetration (British)	Armour Penetration* in mm 457m	1372m	2286m†
2·8cm Spbz 41	coned bore	2·69	0·97	0·84	229	?	1402	90°	66	—	—
								60°	52	—	—
3·7cm Pak 36	?	3·40	1·65	1·17	450	10–15	762	90°	51	—	—
								60°	43	—	—
4·2cm le Pak 41	?	3·69	1·66	1·21	560	10–12	1265	90°	87	—	—
								60°	72	—	—
5cm Pak 38	60	4·75	1·83	1·11	986	12–14	823	90°	78	61	—
								60°	47	40	—
7·5cm Pak 40	48	6·19	2·08	1·25	1425	12–14	792	90°	154	115	83
								60°	115	80	53
7·5cm Pak 41	coned bore	7·49	1·90	1·80	1340	12–14	1210	90°	209	149	—
								60°	171	122	—
7·52cm Pak (r)	—	7·32	2·00	1·40	1710	10	740	90°	120	97	78
								60°	98	79	64
8·8cm Pak 43	71	9·20	2·20	2·05	5000	10	1000	90°	274	211	159
								60°	226	162	114
8·8cm Pak 43/41	71	9·15	2·53	1·98	4380	10	1000	90°	as for Pak 43		
								60°			
8cm Pwk 8H63	?	5·18	3·17·	1·13	630	6–8	525	90°	140 mm at 600m.		

* Figures quoted are for maximum efficiency (i.e. with most effective ammunition).
† Most German sources quote these ranges – which approximate closely to the Allied 500–1500–2500-yard equivalents and may be conversions.
The Allied and German penetration figures are similar!

FIELD AND MEDIUM ARTILLERY

(Guns: *Kanone*; gun-howitzers (*haubitze*); howitzers (*Mörser*).) NB German classifications were 'light' and 'heavy' but the common designation of 'medium' for calibres of about 5–6 inches (150mm) has been used here since it appears in most English texts.

Field and medium artillery in the German army was normally concentrated in Divisional artillery Regiments, although batteries of medium guns and gun-howitzers were also used as corps troops and for coast defence. There were three main calibres, 7·5cm; 10·5cm; 15cm; the ordnance was of conventional design and largely standardised by the beginning of the war in the so-called '18' series.

7·5CM WEAPONS: These light guns (*leichte Feldkanone*) were all designed for horsedrawn transport in one load and were considered as obsolete by 1939. There were three main patterns, the *7·5cm FK16 (n.A)* a modified WW1 vintage gun; *the 7·5cm FK18*, a lighter but shorter range weapon developed in 1930/1 and produced up to 1938; and the *7·5cm FK38*, 144 of which were acquired in 1940 from a cancelled Brazilian order. This was a developed FK18. During the war these guns were issued mainly to low-grade formations including Volksgrenadier and Luftwaffe Field Divisions, and to some static infantry formations.

10·5CM WEAPONS: The standard gun-howitzer of the light batteries was the *10·5cm leichte Feldhaubitze 18 (le FH18)* (Pl. 48) first introduced in 1935. A competent design, its performance was progressively increased by fitting muzzle-brakes and an upgraded recoil mechanism (*le FH18M*), this variant then being further modified with a light split-trail carriage adapted from the 7·5 Pak series (*le FH 18/40*. Pl. 42). This gun, roughly equivalent to the British 25-pounder, was very versatile, firing all types of projectile and being fairly effective even in the anti-tank role at short ranges when firing hollow-charge projectiles.

The other major 10·5cm calibre weapon was the so-called 10cm medium gun (*s 10cm K18*). This was the standard medium long-barrel (flat-trajectory) gun and was used both in the Divisional artillery regiments and by Corps and coast defence troops. It had a fairly massive carriage and limber and was designed for either motor-drawn or horse transport; in the latter case the weapon was hauled in two parts, the carriage, and the barrel on a transporter. Development paralleled the le FH18 series except that the same carriage was used throughout and the *s 10cm K18/40* with a longer barrel did not see series production.

Of the 10·5cm weapons, the le FH18 series was also mounted on a Panzer II chassis for use by the armoured artillery abteilungen as the WESPE (Wasp) with the number Sd Kfz 124 (Pl. 44), and in small numbers on various captured chassis. Experimental trials were also carried out with the complete weapon mounted on a Type IV chassis and capable of firing either from the chassis or dismounted: this *Heuschrecke* (Grasshopper) series never saw production.

15CM WEAPONS: Standard medium field howitzer was the *15cm s18 Schweres Feldhaubitze* (Pl. 43) used by the Divisional artillery and as coast defence. It was a competent but uninspired weapon using the same carriage and limber as

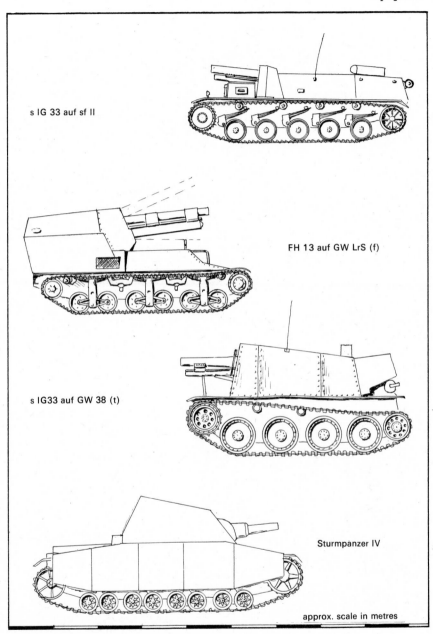

s IG 33 auf sf II

FH 13 auf GW LrS (f)

s IG33 auf GW 38 (t)

Sturmpanzer IV

approx. scale in metres

FIG 22 TYPICAL SP ARTILLERY

the s 10cm K18 series and was developed in parallel with the light equipments. Development culminated in the not very common 15cm s18/43 with muzzle-brake and other improvements. As with the 10·5cm gun-howitzer it was mounted on an SP chassis, the Typ III/IV Geschützwagen, as the HUMMEL (Bumble Bee) with the designation Sd Kfz 165 (Pl. 45). One of the best of the WW1 vintage gun-howitzers, the *15cm sFH13* was also used in this role, mounted on various captured chassis. (Fig. 22.)

HEAVY AND SUPER HEAVY ARTILLERY

The army controlled a wide variety of heavy and super-heavy equipments, most of the latter being static defence or railway guns and really outside the scope of this book. The standard heavy equipments used in the field by Army and Corps troops were the *17cm K18* gun introduced in 1940 and the *21cm Mrs18* introduced in 1939; the latter was a genuine howitzer. Both used the same howitzer carriage (*Mörserlafette*) which was designed to break down into two loads – carriage; barrel on transporter – but could be moved in one piece tactically over short distances (Pl. 46). After 1942, production was concentrated on the 17cm gun.

One should perhaps mention here the *60cm Mörser KARL* a fantastic siege mortar on a fully tracked chassis, six examples of which were used in the Russian campaign. Its chassis was intended only for local manoeuvring and for long distances it was loaded on a Culmeyer multi-wheel transporter.

46 Heavy army artillery was provided mainly by this gun, the 17cm gun on a howitzer carriage. It was normally moved in one piece only for tactical purposes. Prime mover here is a 13 tonne half-track. (IWM)

INFANTRY GUNS (Infanterie Geschütze – IG)

These were peculiar to the German army, being developed from 1927 onwards to meet a requirement for rapid close-support fire, and were operated by special companies within the infantry Regiments. They were of two calibres, 7·5cm and 15cm, and were basically small light howitzers on two-wheeled carriages with box trails. The standard equipments were the *7·5cm leIG18*, a rather novel design by Rheinmetall Borsig with the barrel in a square slipper, and a fixed breech (Pl. 57); its mountain derivative, the *7·5cm le Geb IG18* which broke down for pack carriage; and the *15cm sLG33*, a more conventional gun (Pl. 40) that became the standard close-support howitzer. There were also, from 1944 onwards, improved 7·5cm guns (IG 36 and 37) using conventional, muzzle-braked barrels and light split trail carriages, and towards the end of the war a very efficient dual-purpose gun the *8cm PWK 8H63* was introduced in small numbers as a standard infantry gun/anti-tank weapon. This was an advanced smooth-bore weapon firing both HE and hollow charge shells and, with a muzzle velocity of only 525 metres/second, could penetrate up to 140mm of armour at its fighting range of 600m.

All these equipments were designed for towage by either horse or tractor and for easy manhandling. The sIG33 was also mounted on obsolete Pz I and II chassis for use by Panzer Grenadier Regiments and some were later mounted also on the Czech 38t chassis suitably modified. All these SP guns had light shielding for the crew. (Pl. 22.)

Not normally classed as infantry guns but functioning in that role were the short 7·5cm L24 tank guns which from 1941–on were mounted on various armoured car and armoured half-track chassis for issue to the recce and panzer grenadier abteilungen of the armoured divisions. Carriages included the Sd Kfz 250 and 251 series (Pl. 26), and the Sd Kfz 231 (8 rad) and 234 series (qv).

RECOILLESS GUNS (Leichtegeschütze: LG)

These could be classed as artillery or infantry weapons. They were in essence projectors firing shell and in which the recoil could be almost eliminated by allowing propellant gases to escape through a rear venturi; this allowed a very light carriage but required special cartridges and careful handling by the crew, since to stand behind the gun was fatal! Initially they were intended for use by parachute troops and could be broken down into four or five pack loads.

The first equipment, used experimentally in Crete in 1941, was the *7·5cm LG40* and it proved so useful that it was issued also to infantry units fighting in difficult country. Heavier guns, the *10·5cm LG40* and the *10·5cm LG42 and 43*, were introduced later but in 1943 further development was dropped in favour of high-low pressure guns suitable for a dual role. These were the 7·5cm RfK, a Krupp design weighing only 95lb and firing rifled shot, and the 8cm RfW 43, a similar smooth bore weapon – hence, presumably its W = *Werfer* (mortar) designation.

ANTI-AIRCRAFT ARTILLERY (Flugzeugabwehrkanone = Fla or Flak)

Most German flak artillery was operated by the Luftwaffe, often in close co-operation with the army. The Army did, however, operate flak equipments incorporated as organic units within Divisions and also had a number of Army units (*Heeresflak Abteilungen*). The following guns were used:

2CM FLAK: These were light cannon intended for use by infantry and trans-ported on light two-wheeled carriages (Pl. 49). *The 2cm Flak 30* was introduced in 1935 and an improved version the *2cm Flak 38* supplemented it in 1940. The latter was a good reliable gun with a high effective rate of fire (220 rpm) but effective only to about 6000ft. A quadruple mounted version, the *2cm Flakvierling 38*, was introduced at the same time; it was mounted either on a two-wheeled trailer, for use by the Divisional units or on various half-track and SP chassis for use both by the AA Abteilungen and by the AA units attached to the Panzer Regiments. Main carriages were the 5 and 8 tonne half-tracks and the Type IV tank chassis. *Wirbelwind* (= Whirlwind) was a turreted pattern and *Möbelwagen* (furniture van) had an open fighting compartment (Fig. 17).

3·7CM GUNS: The standard light AA guns in 1939 were the *3·7cm Flak 36 and 37* on two-wheeled trailers. In army use they were incorporated in Tank Regiments on SP chassis (*Ostwind*, Fig. 17 and *Möbelwagen*) and used in separate batteries. They were later supplemented by the improved *3·7cm Flak 43*.

8·8CM GUNS: In army use these equipped the heavy batteries of the Divisional flak abteilungen and also certain Heeresflak abteilungen. They were normally

47. Heavy anti-tank artillery in the Division was mainly provided by the 7·5cm PAK 40, seen here. (WJKD)

Men in the desert

L. to R. General officer in 'correct' tunic and breeches, with leather leggings over canvas-topped shoes. He is wearing the Iron Cross in the standard position. (ii) Man in early issue uniform, with yellow (signals) waffenfarbe. Note the badged pith helmet. (iii) A variation on ii; this man is wearing the issue shirt and breeches with high, laced canvas boots. (iv) A corporal in typical lake-pattern uniform with soft cap, casually worn open-necked tropical tunic with a sweat rag, shorts, and socks rolled down over boots.

Men in camouflage

**L. to R. (i) Paratrooper in early
pattern long jumping smock
over Luftwaffe uniform. Note
rimless jumping helmet. (ii)
Sturmgeschutz crew-man in the
grey variant of 'panzer' uniform. He wears the early forage
cap (feldmutz) and the orange/
red waffenfarbe of the replacement services. (iii) Tank commander in short camouflage
jacket over his panzer uniform.
The camouflage is that designed for street fighting. (iv) S S
infantryman in 'spring' pattern
camouflage smock, and helmet
with foliage camouflage.**

48. An old-pattern leFH18 in 'horse-drawn' guise. Note the box trail, the crew-carrying limber and the invariable rider on each offside horse.   (HU 3894)

modifications of the standard *8·8cm Flak 18, 36, or 37* developed from 1933–on, and were supplemented from 1943 by the genuine dual purpose *8·8cm Flak 41* (Flak equivalent of the 8·8cm Pak 43). They were normally motor-drawn.

HEAVY MORTARS (Werfer)
Learning from Russian experience the Germans were quick to develop various mortar devices for lobbing large shells into enemy positions. These were originally used to lay down smoke – hence the term *Nebelwerfer* (smoke projector) commonly applied to them – but were used mainly for more offensive purposes.
(a) multi-barrelled mortars: Main equipment was the *15cm Nebelwerfer 41* (Pl. 41) a six-barrelled mortar on a simple two-wheeled carriage that incorporated the elevating and traversing gears. It was electrically fired, the barrels firing in succession over about a 90 second period and could fire both HE and smoke. A single-barrelled version, the so-called *Do-Gerät,* was used by airborne troops and there was also a larger calibre five-barrelled variant the *21cm Nebelwerfer 42*; this fired HE only but could be fitted with rails to allow it to fire 15cm calibre projectiles. The most well-known variant of these equipments was the *15cm Panzerwerfer 42* comprising ten barrels of the 15cm pattern mounted on a lightly armoured half-track with a 360 degree traverse. Both the Maultier (qv) and the French Somua vehicles were used as chassis.
(b) Wurfgerät (mortar shell projectors): For speed and simplicity the Germans also designed frames which allowed the heavy mortar ammunition to be fired from its storage crates with somewhat decreased accuracy and much decreased range. The main ones were:
WURFGERÄT 40: A wooden frame capable of firing 28cm and 32cm projectiles.
SCHWERES WURFGERÄT 41: A steel rack version of the above.
28/32CM SCHWERER WURFRAHMEN 40: Basically a locator plate mounted on

the side of an armoured half-track carrier; there were normally six to an Sd Kfz 251 series machine which could still operate in its normal role (Pl. 6).

28/32 NEBELWERFER 41: This was on a 2-wheeled trolley and was thus a cross between a mortar and a simple crate. It was 'laid' like a howitzer but had a short range.

30CM NEBELWERFER 42: Similar to the above, this fired a streamlined rocket projectile up to 5000 metres or more.

In general the proper mortars could fire up to about 8000 metres, the 'racks' only up to about 2500 metres.

Table 6 FIELD & CLOSE SUPPORT ARTILLERY

Piece	Calibre/ Length Rat.	In Travelling Position			Battle Weight (kg)	Rate of Fire (rpm)	Max Range (metres)
		Length (metres)	Width (metres)	Height (metres)			
FIELD 7·5cm K16 n.A.	36	—	—	—	1524	8–10	12300
7·5cm K18	26	5·15	1·83	1·65	1120	8–10	9425
7·5cm K38	34	5·61	1·88	1·58	1380	10–12	11300
10·5cm le FH18	28	6·10	1·98	1·88	1985	6–8	10675
10·5cm le FH18M	28	6·10	1·98	1·88	2040	6–8	12325
10·5cm le FH18/40	28	6·15	2·11	1·83	1800	6–8	12325
10cm SK18	52	8·17	2·26	1·71	5620	6	19075
15cm SFH18	29·6	7·85	2·26	1·71	5512	4	13325
17cm K18	?	12·81	2·83	3·11	17520	40 rph	29600
21cm M18	?	12·81	2·83	3·11	16700	30 rph	16700
Karl					120000	12 rph	6800
INFANTRY GUNS							
7·5cm le IG 18	11·8	2·75	1·60	1·20	400	8–12	3550
7·5cm le Ceb. 36	19·3	4·16	1·19	1·24	750	5–8	9250
15cm sIG 33	11·4	4·30	2·15	1·65	1·75	2–3	4700
LIGHT (Recoilless) GUNS							
7·5cm LG40	15·5	1·97	1·04	0·97	145	8	6800
10·5cm LG42	17·5	2·25	1·46	1·68	485	6–7	7950
10·5cm KG40	13	2·25	1·46	1·68	388	6–7	7950

Table 7 ANTI-AIRCRAFT ARTILLERY

Piece	Calibre/Length Rat.	In Firing Position (barrel lowered)			Weight in kg		Rate of Fire (rpm)		Max Range (in metres)		Muzzle Velocity (in m/s)	
		Length (metres)	Width (metres)	Height (metres)	Battle	On carr.	Cyclic	Practical	Ground	Air	AP	HE
2cm Flak 30	115	4·00	1·81	1·70	450	770	280	120	4800	2200	830	900
2cm Flak 38	112·6	4·08	1·81	1·70	420	750	480	220	4800	2200	830	900
2cm FlakVierl mg 38	112·6	4·33	2·42	2·17	1514	2212	1800	800	4800	2200	830	900
3·7cm Flak 18	98	7·15	2·14	2·21	1750	3560	160	80	6500	3500	770	820
3·7 cm Flak 36 37	98	5·57	2·42	2·13	1550	2400	160	120	6500	3500	770	820
3·7cm Flak 43	89·2	3·49	1·78	1·62	1250	2000	250	180	6500	350	770	820
8·8cm Flak 18	56	7·62	2·31	2·42	5000	7200	—	15-20	14680	10600	795	820
8·8cm Flak 36 37	56	7·62	2·31	2·42	5000	7200	—	15-20	14680	10600	795	820
8·8cm Flak 41	74·3	9·65	2·40	2·36	8000	11200	—	20-25	20000	12350	980	1000

Explosive Devices

The explosive devices used in the German army (Fig. 23) were of four main types:

ANTI-VEHICLE MINES: The Germans used more than forty patterns of anti-vehicle mines during the war, but certain types predominated. Most common was the series of anti-tank mines known as the Tellermines (*Tellerminen*). These differed in detail but the general pattern was a flat cylinder of metal with a sprung lid, designed to be set off by pressure from above. The charge was normally cast TNT or Amatol, and certain marks could be linked by a bridging bar to increase their effectiveness. These mines, initially of zinc and then of steel, could be laid two to four inches below the ground at not less than 7ft maximum distance (to avoid sympathetic detonation) or above ground at 13 to 14ft intervals. They were effective but being made of steel were susceptible to location by mine detectors.

To make location more difficult, and at the same time to conserve precious metal, the Germans from 1943 on developed various non-ferrous mines, also relying on pressure detonation and using amatol as the basic explosive. The first ones were improvised in the field using wooden boxes but purpose-built wood cases were later developed for the *Holzminen* (wooden mines) and *Riegelminen* (bar-mines) series. These were effective once problems of waterproofing had been overcome and were difficult to detect even at close range – a fact the Germans exploited even further by sinking mines in multiple as much as 4 ft underground, with a wooden probe up to ground level as an actuating device. A bakelite-like plastic mushroom-shaped mine, the *Topfmine*, was also developed and used in the later stages of the war.

ANTI-PERSONNEL MINES: The Germans early on developed a very effective series of anti-personnel mines that were heartily loathed by all allied troops. These, known as *S-Minen* or *Schützenminen* (*Schü-minen*), worked on the principle of a shrapnel burst and could be fired by pressure, a pull on a trip wire or electrical control. They were encased first in metal (S-mine 35) and later in wooden or glass cases (S mine 42) or concrete cylinders (*Stockmine* 43). All except the latter, which was sited above ground, could be exposed or buried. A particularly nasty variant used in small quantities but with devestating morale effect was designed to shoot various objects vertically upward if trodden on, with obvious dangers to a soldier's virility.

BOOBY TRAPS: The German combat engineers in particular were very ingenious in devising these, often using standard mines – for example the defusing of one mine might automatically set off another one underneath.

REMOTE-CONTROLLED DEMOLITION VEHICLES (*Funklenkpanzer*): These generally unsuccessful machines resembled small tanks. The original one, much like a miniature British WW1 tank in appearance was the GOLIATH, an electrically driven, expendable vehicle controlled by a cable of up to about 2000 metres in length. In 1944 came the BIV, a fast and more rectangular device that was intended to be driven to its operating area and then controlled by radio. It was not expendable, having a depositable charge in the bows.

Lastly there was the NSU SPRINGER, a petrol-driven tankette with both remote and manual control which also appeared in 1944. All these vehicles

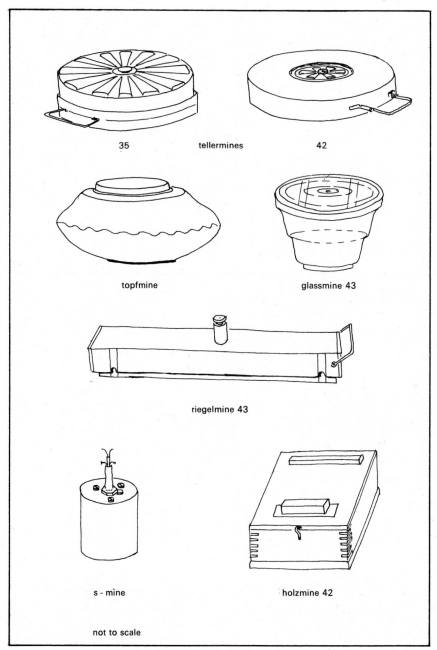

35   tellermines   42

topfmine   glassmine 43

riegelmine 43

s - mine   holzmine 42

not to scale

FIG 23 TYPICAL MINES

were unreliable both in operation and in detonation, and were used only in small quantities.

Specialised Engineer Equipments: Bridges (Brückengerät)

BRIDGES: All Divisional engineer units had light or medium bridging columns for constructing temporary bridges. GHQ units were equipped to put up semi-permanent bridges.

In service at the beginning of the war was a miscellany of fairly old equipments such as the *Brückengerät C*, a small wooden pontoon bridge with built-up superstructure that could be used in a variety of roles, with a maximum weight of just over five tonnes. For most of the war, however, there were two standard bridging equipments in use by the Divisions, the *Brückengerät K* and the *Brückengerät B*, the bridging columns being identified by the appropriate initial letter.

The Brückengerät K was the standard bridge of the armoured engineers. It was a box or bow girder bridge mounted on three-compartment pontoons and able to be laid in sections two, three or four girders wide. The official maximum rating was 16 tonnes load.

The Brückengerät B was a normal pattern of pontoon bridge using a flat-bed superstructure on undecked steel pontoons and having a maximum load in excess of 20 tonnes in most of its forms. It was normally issued to Infantry and Panzer Grenadier Divisions but was sometimes allocated to armoured Divisions in addition to Brückengerät K for special tasks. A third, lighter pattern, *Brückengerät D*, was used by some mechanised infantry pioneer platoons in the divisional infantry Regiments. It was a pontoon and girder bridge with a maximum load of 9 tonnes. In addition, all engineer units were trained to build improvised light bridges and carried a supply of wood, etc for this purpose.

GHQ bridging units, normally allocated to Armies, had heavy structures normally with massive decked pontoons supporting wide, built-up spans. A variety was in use, the most common being the ex-Czech Herbert bridge and the *Brückengerät S*; both these had a distributed loading (tracked vehicles) of over 24 tonnes.

Note on Communications Equipment

German communications equipment was good in general and fairly similar to its allied equivalents. Field telephones were widely used by all arms in static positions, connected through mobile telephone exchanges, and infantry and motorised troops were issued down to company level with two basic pack wireless sets (transmitter/receivers). These were the d2 (Pl. 59) with a notional range of 4km for RT and 15km for WT use; and the b1 with ranges of 10km (RT) and 25km (WT). More powerful transmitters of up to 100 watts and ranges of up to 200km were in use by mobile units and HQs.

Camouflage

Starting from very simple origins, the German army developed the use of tactical vehicle camouflage to a very high standard, often using a distemper-like paint over a basic finish so that colour schemes could be quickly changed as circumstances required. The whole subject is complicated enough to fill a book on its own and only basic notes can be given here.

As a general rule, all vehicles and weapons left the factories painted in a single overall base colour. Up to about February 1943 this was the so-called Panzer Grey, a darkish grey, for European sectors and a dark yellow (dunkelgelb) for the more arid fronts (eg Africa, S. Russia). From 1943 on, the most common colour was the dark yellow although some western front vehicles were still turned out in grey or dark green (dunkelgrün). Units in the field were then issued with various shades of paint, greens, browns and wine red (bordeauxrot) being most used, with white for winter work. These could be either brushed or sprayed on and although there were approved patterns, results often varied widely from these. Mottle or snaking lines of one colour were the most common, green or red-brown on yellow, and light green on dark green being for obvious reasons very popular combinations. Non-AFV vehicles tended to be all grey or yellow and towed guns were also usually one colour; grey, yellow and dark earth were all common and such weapons tended to rely on camouflage netting to escape observation.

One slight complication was the use of *Zimmerit,* an anti-magnetic paste used in 1942–4 on the Russian front especially to lessen the risk from infantry-thrown sticky bombs. This had a ridged appearance and a neutral grey tint; it was not so effective when overpainted but this was often done when tactical camouflage considerations required.

49. **Light flak: A** Krupp LH243 truck towing the standard 2cm light AA/AT gun on its travelling carriage. Note the Luftwaffe registration. (MH 185)

6
The Men and their Accoutrements

As in all armies of the period, the Germans differentiated sharply between infantry and other specialist troops such as tank crews. The difference extended even to the pattern of uniform and small arms carried by the men concerned but the German definition of infantry differed also from that of the Allies. In particular, engineers and pioneers in the German army were classified as combatant and were often elite troops expected to be able to handle specialised equipment while leading an assault. They normally controlled the flame-throwers for example and even in horse-drawn divisions were at least partly motorised. Oddly enough, the most effective fighting infantry, the Panzer Grenadiers, were officially classed as belonging to the armoured arm, although they were equipped and fought in normal infantry fashion. This chapter illustrates some typical unit organisations, with notes, describes the uniform dress of all arms and details the standard patterns of infantry weapons included within organic units.

Infantry Formations

As with the allies the basis of all infantry formations was the *Kompanie* (company) divided into *Züge* (s. Zug) or platoons, each Zug being split into three or four sections. The general pattern of organisation was similar for all types but as Fig. 24 shows, exact allocation of weapons varied both with the type of Division and with the period of the war. As the war progressed, there tended especially to be a larger concentration of both short and long range automatic weapons than in equivalent allied units. Additionally the German policy of decentralising heavy infantry weapons meant that all units down to company level had their own allocation of heavy machine guns and mortars; from 1941 on this arrangement was gradually streamlined as first the MG34/42 machine guns and then the 8·1cm mortars were standardised for both rifle companies and support units; and the old distinction between light and heavy machine guns virtually disappeared.

In the field the various branches of the infantry and other arms were distinguished mainly by the coloured piping, or *Waffenfarbe*, that denoted their arm of service (see p. 142), and in the case of the Waffen SS additionally by modified symbols placed rather differently from those of the ordinary army. Only the paratroops wore a distinctive pattern of dress and this usually comprised smocks, jumping boots and other items particular to their trade. Deutsches Afrika Korps, it is true, had a special tropical dress initially but this, in modified form, was later adopted as a summer uniform for the climatically hotter fronts.

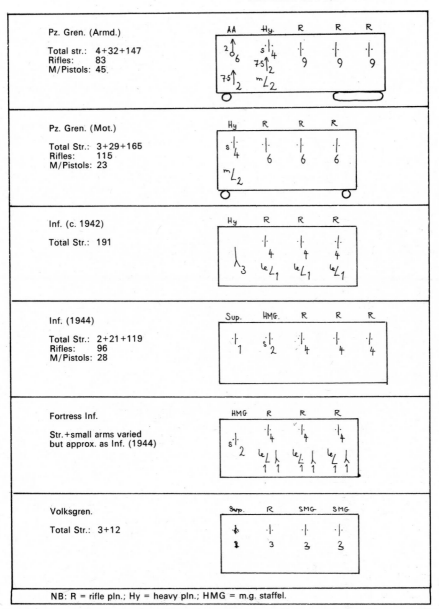

FIG 24 TYPICAL INFANTRY COMPANIES

50. Waffen SS infantry in field uniform with early pattern tunics. Note
the 'battle kit' consisting of haversack, respirator case and
entrenching tool slung from the belts, and the SS eagle and
divisional armband together with black shoulder straps. The left-
hand man has a Luger pistol and what appears to be a 'dreibein'
tripod. (MH 225)

Specialist Formations

Artillery and other 'towed weapon' crews, and all the administrative formations
were usually classed as infantry so far as equipment was concerned; indeed they
received infantry training and even such unoffensive units as the field post
offices had their allocations of small arms and machine guns for local defence.
Panzer troops and self-propelled gun crews who spent most of their time riding
in the confined spaces of their vehicles had their own patterns of uniform and
were armed almost exclusively with short range automatic weapons for local
defence.

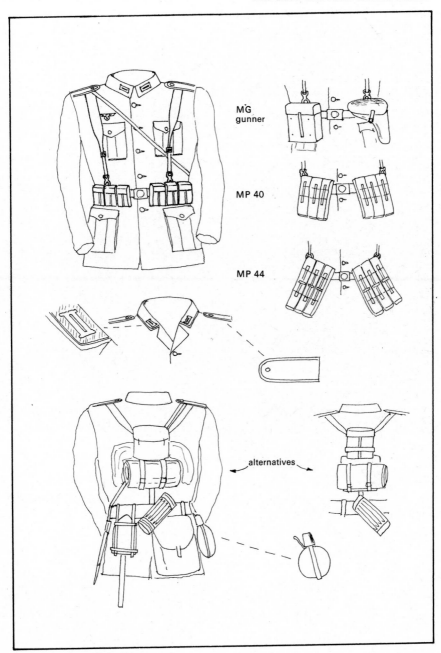

MG
gunner

MP 40

MP 44

alternatives

FIG 25 INFANTRYMAN'S KIT

51. Combat engineers crossing a stream, using the small inflatable boat. Note foliage camouflage. (MH 486)

Infantry Uniforms and Basic Equipment

The standard dress of the German army comprised, as in all armies, four main patterns. First there were the various forms of parade or walking-out dress, all fairly elaborate and designed for morale and propaganda purposes. Then there was the field uniform for everyday work; lastly there were the specialised clothes both for fighting purposes – eg camouflage smocks – and for fatigue duties and other physically dirty work.

BASIC FIELD UNIFORM

The basic uniform, on which all others were modelled, was the field uniform, most elements of which were common to both army and Waffen SS. It was designed for comfort combined with practicability and comprised a tunic (*bluse*), trousers and either calf-length leather boots (the so-called jackboots) or ankle boots, together with appropriate headgear and underwear.

The tunic on issue at the outbreak of war was a long, good quality wool and rayon jacket with four pleated patch pockets and a shirt-type collar which buttoned close up to the neck (Fig. 25). The tunic colour was a warm green – weathering to grey-green – that the Germans called '*feldgrau*' (field grey) and its collar and shoulder straps were originally covered in a bluish green imitation velvet, though by 1939 most new issue uniforms omitted this. The shoulder-straps were also piped round their edges with the appropriate Waffenfarbe colour. The tunic buttons were dull grey and the 'standard' insignia comprised a stylised German eagle above the right breast pocket and stylised embroidered patches on each side of the collar (Fig. 25). These patches, obviously derived

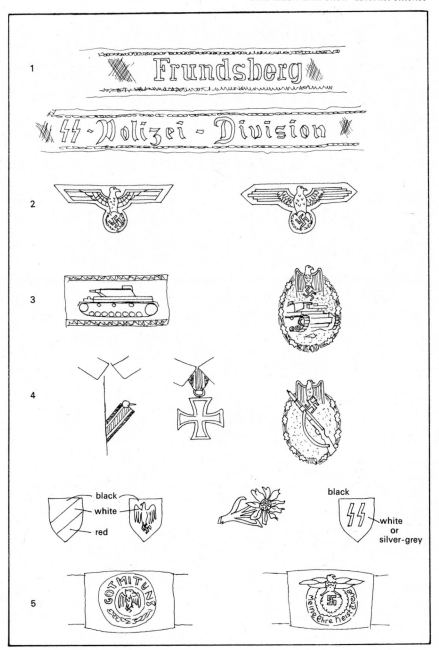

FIG 26 TYPICAL INSIGNIA

52. An assault squad. The middle man is operating a pack-type
flamethrower while the left one has a Kampfpistol. Note the full kit
except for back pack, and the tricolour shield on their helmet sides.
The objects in slings are shelter quarters.   (MH 199)

from the original Prussian 'Doppel-Litzen' or lace ornamentation, consisted of
a double bar in silver-grey thread with a central strip of the appropriate Waffenfarbe colour. The collar could be worn open or buttoned, a green knitted under-
shirt with collar being provided for everyday wear. SS troops wore a different
pattern of eagle (Fig. 26) on their left sleeve instead of the breast, and replaced
the right hand collar patch with a dark trapezium patch bearing the SS double
lightning flash or else by Divisional Insignia; the left hand patch was a similar
trapezium with rank insignia. Some SS Units, and a few others, also had the
unit name or initial embroidered on a band just above the left cuff (Fig. 26).
Some SS men had a pattern of tunic that differed from the army pattern and was
based on the pre-war SS parade uniform.

The standard pattern of tunic was issued and worn right up to the end of the
war but from 1943 on it was supplemented by a much poorer-quality one with
no pleats to the pockets and with piping only on the shoulder straps. This had
six buttons instead of five and the collar was designed to lie open if required,
with shaped lapels (Fig. 25). There was also a 1944 pattern resembling British
battledress. It was single-breasted, with a turned-down collar and patch-pockets;
the wrists and waist-band were close fitting and it had no skirts. It was used in
some numbers.

With the tunic was worn trousers originally of a blue-grey colour, usually
tucked into the tops of the leather marching boots. From 1942/3 onwards, in
order to save cost and material, field grey trousers of the same material as the
jacket were introduced and from late 1943 on, full-length trousers worn with
ankle-boots and canvas 'gaiters' similar to the British pattern became fairly

common. These had been introduced earlier in tropical kit with the Afrika Korps and found serviceable so that their issue was logical when leather was in short supply.

NB – In all cases, but especially as the war went on, the field grey colour tended to vary widely with weathering and cleaning; although always described, and usually shown, as a warm green, the most commonly found colour was more of a green-tinged slate grey and even new tunics towards the end of the war appear to have been dyed this colour. Certainly they faded quickly to it.

HEADGEAR: Standard headgear was the distinctively shaped, flared-rim steel helmet usually referred to by allied sources as the 'coal-scuttle' helmet (Pl. 55). This was a one-piece pressed steel design made in five sizes with a leather liner inside and was painted dull grey. It was developed from the later World War I variety and at the beginning of the war many 1916-pattern helmets, distinguishable by the provision of lugs for a facepiece, were on issue. The standard 1936-pattern one was smaller, lighter and initially decorated with a red-black-white shield painted on the right side and a similar black shield with a stylised white or silver eagle and swastika on the left. (Fig. 26.) These were usually omitted in later war years. The helmet was an efficient combat headpiece, unlike the contemporary British design which could result in a broken neck from blast effect, and after 1940 was often unofficially provided with a wide rubber band or a net slipped over it which could be used to affix foliage camouflage.

Apart from the helmet, all ranks were issued with the '*Feldmütze*' or forage cap, a fore-and-aft style similar to the British pattern. This could also be used

53. A light machine gun team in camouflage smocks and helmet
    covers going through a wood. Note the ammunition carrier with
    no rifle. (MH 1923)

as a cap-comforter under the helmet and was of field grey cloth with the cloth eagle and a red-white-black cockade on the front and a piping of waffenfarbe colour; SS men sometimes had the eagle on the left side with a stylised metal or metallic thread death's head at the front. From 1943 on, this cap was replaced by the *'Einheitsmütze'* (standard cap), a peaked cap based on the Afrika Korps cap and again carrying national insignia. It was soft-topped and its sides could be folded down and buttoned under the chin in cold weather. Mountain troops had their own variation (Pl. 54) which differed slightly (*Gebirgsmütze*). Genuine cap comforters were also issued.

OVERCOATS: All ranks, including officers, were issued with a field grey topcoat (*Mantel*) which was officially intended to go with their parade uniform but was also extensively used on active service. This was a long double-breasted garment buttoning up to the neck and, originally, having a dark green collar for the army and a plain one for the SS. General rank officers had an open, lapelled collar with red revers (army) or pale grey revers (Waffen SS). It had a short, buttoned half-belt but the normal service leather belt was usually worn either completely outside or slotting through two slits at the rear. Epaulettes in the same style as those on the uniform jacket were worn.

Other ranks were also issued with a shelter quarter of rubberised cloth which served both for constructing bivouacs (Pl. 10) and as a rain-cape; for the latter purpose the soldier wore it as a poncho with his head through a hole in the middle and often secured the flapping ends to his trousers above the knee with thongs. Officers often had a black or brown leather coat and various patterns of anorak and heavy coat were issued at times to soldiers in severe climatic conditions.

EQUIPMENT: The full layout of equipment carried by a normal private is shown in Fig. 25. It comprised a blackened leather belt and harness which supported at the front various patterns of blackened leather ammunition pouches and/or holsters, the pattern depending on the weapon carried; at the back a hide or canvas pack, a canteen and slings for the greatcoat or shelter quarter. Hung from the belt were a bayonet frog, a gas respirator container (a fluted, grey-green metal cylinder) and an entrenching tool. Normal equipment also included a small haversack and a water bottle. In battle, naturally enough, part of the equipment was often left off and what remained was often hung from the belt.

PARADE UNIFORMS

These were strictly a peace-time issue and were of similar pattern to the field uniform but gaudier, since they were intended for morale and propaganda purposes. There were several varieties for different duties but the main ones were the *Ausgehanzug*, or walking-out uniform, and the *Paradeanzug*.

The walking out uniform comprised a smarter version of the field tunic with blue-green trimming to collar, cuffs and shoulder-straps and having waffenfarbe piping not only round these trimmings but also along the front edges of the coat; long blue-grey trousers piped down the side with the appropriate colour, high shoes and a leather belt with a sword (portepee) (senior NCOs) or decorated bayonet (JNCOs and other ranks). Decorations and awards were worn and a coloured tassel (troddel) on the frog or sword hilt

Men in winter

L. to R. Top row: (i) Motor-cyclist in white parka with hood over a standard issue fur cap. He has the respirator-like face mask sometimes used under very severe conditions. (ii) Motor-cyclist with fur hat and toque. (iii) Man in the heavy rubberised coat issued to motor-cycle troops; bottom row: (iv) Infantryman in white cloth smock and trousers with whitened helmet. (v) Infantry captain showing hooded smock with rank insignia. He is wearing the einheitsmutze with the flaps folded down to form a toque. (vi) Infantry officer in sheepskin coat and service cap.

Men in the field

L. to R. (i) **A panzer officer in the black tank-man's uniform with short, double-breasted jacket and early-pattern beret. He is wearing officer's pattern brown leather belt and has the pink panzer waffenfarbe piping; (ii) An infantry private in 1943-pattern tunic, camouflage trousers, late-pattern gaiters and ankle boots. He has the Einheitsmutze and typical 'combat kit' consisting of the small haversack hung from his belt and supporting a mess tin. (iii) Infantryman in 1936-pattern uniform but with his tunic neck unbuttoned. Unusual but sometimes found in combat was the combination of regular ammunition pouches with those for long sub-machine gun magazines. (iv) SS Infantryman wearing a shelter-quarter as a poncho in 'spring' pattern camouflage.**

54. MG42 being fired as LMG on its bipod by mountain troops. Note Gebirgsmütze and Eidelweiss badge. (MH 308)

indicated rank for officers and NCOs and the specific unit for other ranks. A high peaked Service cap was worn with this uniform. The parade uniform was similar but was worn with helmet, jackboots and cartridge pouches where appropriate. Pre-war, regimental or unit numbers were often worn on the shoulder straps of this dress and even on the field uniform but the practice was discontinued for security purposes early in the war.

OFFICERS: Officers normally wore similar uniforms to their men though of rather better quality, and distinguished by the appropriate rank insignia. Except under fire it was common to find officers wearing their peaked service caps in the field and field grade officers and above frequently wore riding boots, breeches and a smartly cut field jacket.

TROPICAL DRESS

It is difficult to describe any general pattern of tropical dress since Afrika Korps, like the British 8th Army, adopted distinctly non-standard dress in many cases. Original issue appears to have been an open-collared pattern of field tunic in khaki green with a khaki shirt, shorts, knee-stockings or long, laced canvas boots; alternatively, long baggy trousers were issued for wear with ankle boots. Headgear was originally a colonial-type pith helmet with appropriate cockades but this was soon changed to either the fore-and-aft cap or to a visored soft-topped cap. The dies used were by no means fade-resistant and all uniforms tended to bleach to a neutral cloth colour. After 1942, the later-pattern uniform – Einheitsmütze, open-necked jacket, long trousers and ankle boots – was adopted as standard summer dress for all warm fronts; insignia for both army and Waffen SS (1943 on) were as on the field uniform. It was quite normal on active service to find elements of both uniforms worn in combination.

CAMOUFLAGE UNIFORMS

Particularly during the last years of the war, extensive use was made of both camouflage smocks and complete camouflage uniforms. In general, they were used mainly by Waffen SS (all-arms); panzer grenadiers; paratroops and mountain troops but line infantry frequently had special winter clothing. Winter smocks and trousers were white in colour, at first merely of thin cloth for concealment but later made of wind and waterproof material and incorporating a hood. They were normally worn over the field uniform and most were reversible, with a brown/green camouflage pattern on the other side. This reversibility was a feature of German camouflage dress, complete camouflage suits being later adopted which had a 'spring and summer' pattern on one side and an 'autumn' pattern with a reddish tinge on the other. Waffen SS had a different pattern from army troops and their tank crews were sometimes issued with camouflaged coveralls or jackets.

RANK BADGES AND OTHER INSIGNIA

Rank was normally indicated by decorations on the uniform shoulder straps: ORs were plain with piping; NCOs had a thick strip of aluminium or grey silk braid inside the piping with various pips denoting exact rank; officers had the straps almost covered with braid or, for higher ranks, with intertwined cords. Junior NCOs had also sleeve badges on their left sleeves and SS units additionally used the left hand collar patch to show rank. Special dulled arm patches were designed for use with camouflage uniforms but in service normal insignia were often worn, even at the risk of compromising concealment. This tendency to wear bright insignia even if it negated the value of dull-coloured uniforms was a constant feature of German army life. It has been said that the German soldier was less willing than his allied counterpart to engage in close combat and that his morale had to be encouraged by the issue of special insignia showing prowess in this field. Whether or not this is true, the average soldier certainly liked to display his awards and a number of close-combat badges of various types were produced (examples in Fig. 26). Other coloured badges were those for marksmanship, general decorations for bravery (eg the Iron Cross) and the various Divisional and unit or Campaign names sometimes worn as armbands especially by the SS. They were frequently worn with the field uniform on active service.

Paratroops, Mountain Troops, Panzer Troops and Other Services

*PARATROOPS: were officially Luftwaffe and originally wore a luftwaffe blue-grey jump suit or coverall, resembling a boiler suit with four large pockets. Over this was a long grey-green smock that could be kilted up for jumping; this smock was later (1942 on) replaced by a similar camouflaged smock and

---

*There were in the order of battle 1 or 2 SS "Parachute Battalions" but these were probably nominal only.

later still (1943 on) the uniform was generally replaced by infantry-type clothing consisting of a shorter, camouflaged smock, luftwaffe trousers in grey-blue, and ankle boots. The paratroops always had a light, almost rimless helmet which also acted as a crash helmet when jumping, and this was retained until the end of the war, usually with a camouflage cover. Similar covers were also used by other arms.

MOUNTAIN TROOPS: wore the standard pattern uniform adapted to their particular circumstances. Specifically they always had a peaked field cap (gebirgsmütze) somewhat similar to the later einheitsmütze and normally wore climbing boots with puttees rather than jackboots. For severe weather conditions they were issued with a green waterproof thigh-length double breasted jacket and/or a long reversible camouflage smock.

PANZER TROOPS: Mechanised troops other than infantry wore a uniform adapted to their particular needs of operating in a restricted space. It consisted basically of a short double-breasted jacket with full-length trousers and ankle boots, although shoes were sometimes worn instead of the latter. The normal belt was worn but without harness, and headgear ranged from a black beret during the early stages of the war, through the normal patterns of fore-and-aft cap and Einheitsmütze. Insignia were normal except that collar patches for all troops were black with a traditional aluminium death's head (*Totenkopf*) device. Uniform colour was black for tank and armoured car crews, and field grey for assault gun and specialised SP artillery (eg anti-tank unit) crews. The same pattern of uniform was later (end 1943 on) issued in camouflage material, a style used mainly by the Waffen SS.

LUFTWAFFE AND KRIEGSMARINE UNITS SERVING WITH THE ARMY: Luftwaffe field Divisions normally wore field uniforms in the Luftwaffe grey-blue but with ordinary infantry equipment. Flak batteries also wore Luftwaffe uniform but often substituted coveralls in blue or rust-brown when in action. Kriegsmarine units utilised army pattern uniforms almost exclusively with minor modifications to insignia.

Infantry Weapons

Infantry weapons described in this section include small arms, mortars, anti-tank rifles and projectors, and the various grenades.

SMALL ARMS

Infantry small arms can be divided into four main categories: pistols or revolvers; rifles; machine pistols (roughly analagous to the British sten gun); and machine guns. The Germans excelled in the design and production of semi and fully automatic weapons and, as the war went on, the proportion of such weapons in each infantry unit was stepped up and the rate of fire, particularly of machine guns, was increased. This was especially so after the early Russian campaigns showed that the rifle was not ideal for mobile warfare and that versatile short range weapons with a high rate of fire were needed for assault and close range street fighting. As a consequence it appeared that great quantities of varying ammunition types would be needed and, to ease the supply problems the German designers concentrated on standardisation and versatility; the outstanding

131

results were the two main machine guns which, with minor adaptations, could function as light and heavy machine guns against ground troops and as anti-aircraft weapons. Statistical details of all weapons are given on p. 144.

PISTOLS: There were two main pistols, the Luger (Pistole 08) and the Walther (Pistole 38). Both were semi-automatic and recoil-operated, using 9mm ammunition. The Luger, of World War 1 vintage, was made in standard and long-barrelled versions, the latter having provision for clipping on a stock, with a rear sight graduated to 800 metres; it could thus be used as an 'ersatz' machine pistol in emergency. The Walther was more modern and produced as a pistol only. The Germans also used signal pistols (*Leichtpistolen*) analagous to the British Verey Light pistol, but made them adaptable to take special grenades (then called *Kampfpistolen*) and even a special close-range hollow charge projectile (as the *Sturmpistole*). Both these modifications could be quickly removed to allow use of the weapon in its original role.

55. MG34 in the heavy role on its adjustable tripod. The men have battle kit only. (MH 9406)

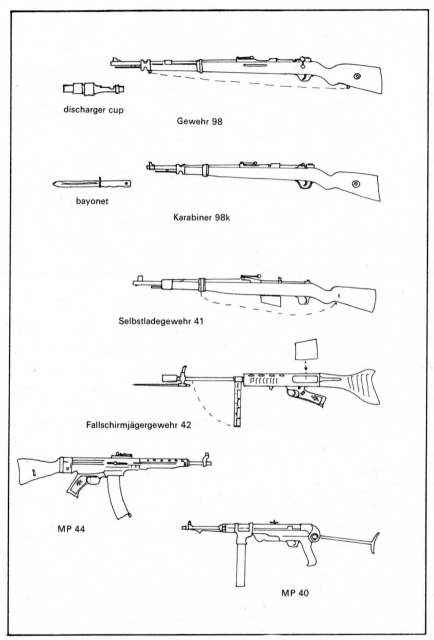

discharger cup

Gewehr 98

bayonet

Karabiner 98k

Selbstladegewehr 41

Fallschirmjägergewehr 42

MP 44

MP 40

FIG 27 SMALL ARMS

RIFLES: The standard issue rifle (Fig. 27) at the beginning of the war was the model 98, dating from before the First World War. This traditional, bolt operated Mauser-pattern weapon was made as the rifle (*Gewehr* 98), a long barrelled carbine of about the same length (*Karabiner* 98*b*) and a short barrelled carbine (*Karabiner* 98*k*). The weapons had generally similar performances the main difference being that the carbines had a cavalry-type sling at the side, instead of underneath as in a rifle. The rear sight was graduated from 100 to 2000 metres and the weapon could fire grenades from a cup or spigot launcher that could be attached to the muzzle. A sword bayonet was provided. A modified version of this weapon in shortened form and with a folding stock was produced for parachute troops as the *Gewehr* 33/40. Calibre was 7·92mm.

The other main rifles used by the line infantry were the *Selbstladegewehr* 41 and its development the *Selbstladegewehr* 43. As can be guessed from their names, these were semi-automatic and were gas-operated, with a magazine holding two standard five-round clips of rifle ammunition. They could be fitted with telescopic sights and were normally issued one per rifle section for use by snipers.

The only other standard rifle used in quantity was the *Fallschirmjaeger-gewehr* 42 designed for parachute troops. This was not a true rifle, being an automatic weapon, gas-operated with provision for single and continuous shots and having a permanent folding bipod; it could thus be used as a light machine gun or machine pistol and in addition was fitted with a bayonet for assault work. Calibre was 7·92mm.

56. Infantry manoeuvring a 3·7cm light anti-tank gun during an early campaign. (MH 1895)

MACHINE PISTOLS: These weapons (Fig. 27), analagous to allied sub machine guns, are commonly referred to as Schmeissers although few of the standard weapons were in fact designed or built by that firm. There were two major types of which the first, the MP38 and MP40 were very similar except for their stocks. These guns, originally designed for parachute troops, were in general use for close range fighting at the outbreak of war. They fired standard 9mm calibre pistol ammunition from a 32-round magazine, had a short range and tended to jam if fired for bursts of more than 5–10 rounds. They were issued to unit commanders and their deputies, and towards the end of the war were also allocated to rifle sections on the basis of two per section, and to special machine pistol (assault) platoons.

The *MP43/1* and the *MP44* were developed as a result of the early Russian campaigns and the obvious need for a better assault weapon than the MP38. Both were of 7·92mm calibre taking standard 'short' rifle ammunition and being gas operated with provision for single and continuous shots. They were intended to combine the best features of rifles and machine pistols in one weapon and were officially known as *Sturmgewehr* – assault rifles. They were surprisingly accurate up to about 800 metres but had the disadvantage that they were made from metal pressings and could only be partially stripped in the field. The most common type was the MP44 which could be fitted with the standard rifle grenade discharger cup and was also issued to tank crews for local defence; for this and for sniping it could be fitted with an ingenious 'bent barrel' extension allowing the shot to be fired at an angle of $32\frac{1}{2}$ degrees from the line of

57. A 7·5cm LG18 light infantry gun with its crew in camouflage smocks and helmet covers. (STT 3081)

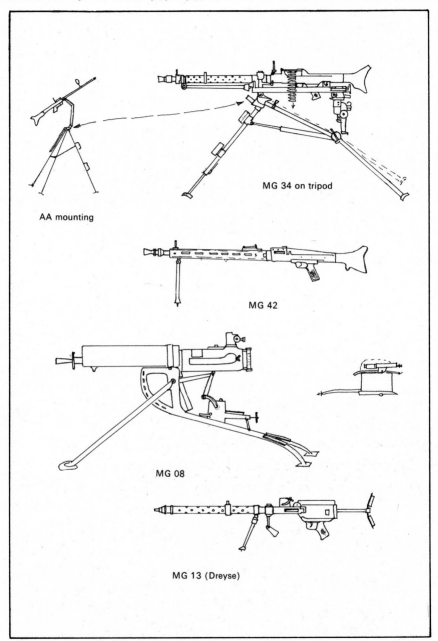

MG 34 on tripod

AA mounting

MG 42

MG 08

MG 13 (Dreyse)

FIG 28 COMMON MACHINE GUNS

sight. Special deflection sights were provided for this; otherwise the two weapons were very similar.

It should be noted that various older models, of both Schmeisser and Bergmann manufacture, were also in use in 1939 but these were phased out and are not important.

MACHINE GUNS (*Maschinengewehr*): Commonly known to the British as Spandaus, presumably in memory of the WW1 aircooled guns manufactured at that town, this class of weapon was fairly varied. In 1939 the German army had in use a number of fairly old equipments, notably the MG 08 heavy water-cooled machine gun and light machine guns of the 08/15 (water-cooled), 08/18 (air-cooled) and MG13 (air-cooled) patterns. Of these only the MG08, a heavy, tripod mounted weapon used by some infantry divisions (Fig. 28), and the MG13, often known as the *Dreyse* gun and used mainly in early AFVs, remained in anything like large-scale use. The others were quickly replaced in the main fighting units by the first of two standard weapons, the MG34, which came into service early in 1939. This (Pl. 55; Fig. 28) was an extremely versatile equipment, the first machine-gun to be designed as a genuine multi-purpose weapon. Of 7·92mm calibre, air-cooled, with provision for single and continuous shots and firing standard short rifle ammunition in 50-round belts, it could be used with its bipod as a light machine gun and on a special tripod mounting as a heavy weapon. In both roles it was superior to contemporary allied weapons both in rate and weight of fire and it could additionally be used for anti-aircraft defence either on a modified tripod or on a special AA tripod (*MG34 Dreibein*); where belt feed was inconvenient, a drum magazine could be used as an alternative. It remained the standard tank machine gun until the

58. Raketenwerfer 43, anti-tank projector.   (MH 399)

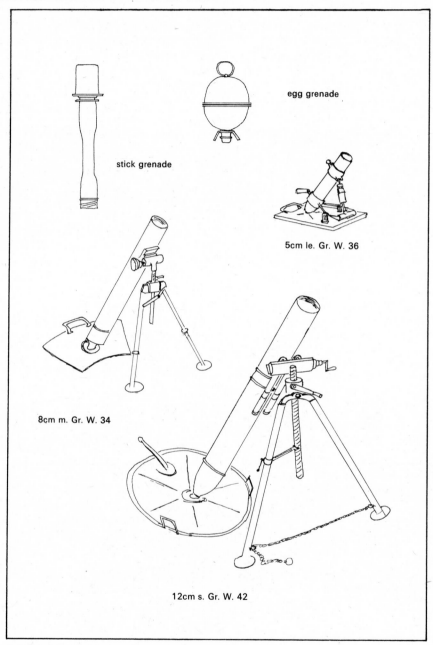

egg grenade

stick grenade

5cm le. Gr. W. 36

8cm m. Gr. W. 34

12cm s. Gr. W. 42

FIG 29 GRENADES and MORTARS

war's end but was gradually supplanted in infantry use by the famous MG42, generally considered the best machine gun of World War 2.

The *MG42* (Fig. 28, Pl. 54) was built mainly from metal pressings and at first sight appeared so crude that it was seriously underestimated by allied intelligence. It was in fact, a first class equipment with all the versatility of its predecessor except that it fired only continuous shot – but at the very high cyclic rate of fire of 1200 rounds a minute. As with the MG34, it was issued to infantry sections as a light machine gun and, complete with tripod and carriage, to heavy machine gun sections and platoons. The designation 'medium machine gun' in this role was a purely allied one and was not recognised by the Germans. Its only drawbacks were that the square body section made it unsuitable for fitting as a tank machine gun in the existing mantlets and that the torque caused by the high rate of fire made the muzzle lift if the gun was fired in long bursts. The chromium barrel required changing less often.

OTHER GUNS: During various crises a number of aircraft guns were also modified for ground use as the MG15. These were improvisations with clip-on bipods and added stocks, and were not very effective. They were used mainly in multiple mounts for anti-aircraft protection.

MORTARS

The Germans started the war with 5cm (approx 2in.) and 8·1cm (approx 3in.) calibre trench mortars (Fig. 29) of roughly equivalent performance to the similar British equipments; unlike the British, however, they quickly realised the uselessness of the 5cm equipment and by 1943 had developed a shortened and lightened version of the 8·1cm mortar to take its place in infantry platoons.

59. Standard pack wireless set for unit signals. (MH 298)

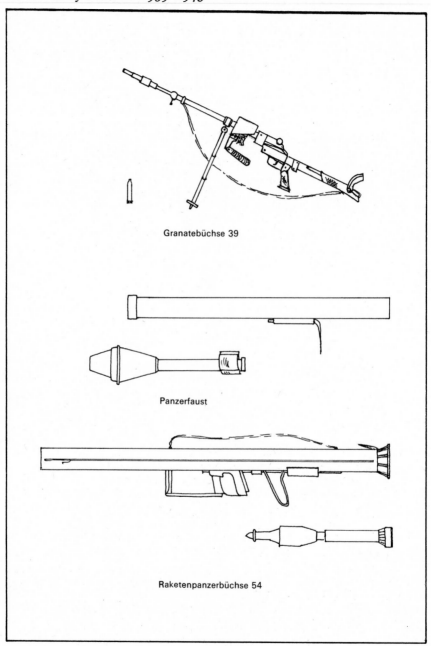

Granatebüchse 39

Panzerfaust

Raketenpanzerbüchse 54

FIG 30 INFANTRY ANTI-TANK WEAPONS

They also learnt quickly from the Russians, first using captured examples of the big Russian 12cm mortar and then copying it for heavy work; its mobility was greatly improved by the provision of a two-wheeled trolley fitted with pneumatic tyres and it was issued to heavy companies of both line infantry and panzer grenadier regiments.

In general German mortars were not markedly different in performance from equivalent allied types but they were imaginatively used, provided in greater quantity for infantry formations, and made as mobile as possible, thus becoming effective close support weapons. Medium and heavy mortars, usually of 10cm calibre, were also used extensively by Army and Corps troops- for smoke and chemical warfare; while considerable use was made of multiple equipments, details of which will be found under 'Artillery' (Ch. 5).

INFANTRY ANTI-TANK WEAPONS

As with most contemporary armies, the Germans started the war with small calibre anti-tank rifles (Fig. 30) (*Panzerbüchsen*) of 7·92cm calibre, in particular the Panzerbüchse 38 and 39. Neither these, nor the 2cm Solothurn anti-tank rifle proved very effective and by the beginning of 1944 design effort was concentrated on anti-tank grenade launchers (the *Panzerfaust* or *Faustpatrone* series) and rocket launchers (*Raketenpanzerbüchsen*). One anti-tank rifle was converted to take a rifle grenade launcher as the *Granatebüchse* 39 but the main infantry equipment in 1944 and after was the series of Panzerfaust devices ranging from the *Panzerfaust Klein* 30 (*Faustpatrone* 1) and *Panzerfaust* 30 (Faustpatrone 2), which had effective ranges of only 30 metres, up through the *Panzerfaust* 60 to the *Panzerfaust* 100, the latter being said to be effective at up to 150 metres. All these were basically composed of a steel launching tube containing a propellant charge. This fired a hollow-charge, bulbous-nosed grenade equipped with spring-loaded folding stabilising fins that were released as it left the tube.

The *Raketenpanzerbüchse* 54, on the other hand, otherwise known as *Ofenrohr* (stove-pipe) or *Panzerschreck* (tank-terror) was a true bazooka, firing rocket-propelled hollow-charge projectiles; it was sometimes fitted with a small shield and had an effective range of 120 metres. Its stable companion, the *Raketenwerfer* 43 (Pl. 58) was in effect a small recoilless gun on a two-wheeled carriage, fitted with a crew shield and claimed to be effective up to about 700 metres.

A NOTE ON GRENADES

The Germans used mainly the so-called 'stick-grenades', consisting of a warhead mounted on the end of a short stave. They were either thrown overhand or lobbed, although the latter action was commoner for the egg-shaped grenades (*Eihandgranaten*) that were also used. The rifle grenade was different again and resembled a small shell. It required not only a grenade discharger cup (*Gewehrgranatgerät*) but also a different method of firing since it was not fired on a flat trajectory.

Waffenfarbe Colours (used on uniforms and often on signs, etc., belonging to a particular unit).

line infantry (grenadiere)	white
mountain	light green
jaeger	light green
Panzer grenadiere	grass green
reconnaissance (fusilier)	golden yellow ⎫ under classification of
cavalry units	golden yellow ⎬ mobile (schnelle) originally
tank, SP artillery	⎫
armoured reconnaisance	⎬ pink*
ground artillery	⎫
army flak	⎬ red
engineers	black
smoke troops	maroon
signals	lemon yellow
supply	light blue
medical	darkish blue
veterinary	carmine red
provost and recruiting	orange-red
Wehrmachtbeamten	dark green
technical officers	orange-red
Army	red
Waffen SS	dark grey
SS	brown

* Certain units – some Waffen SS and 24 Panzer Divisions in particular—retained the old calvalry/Schnelle truppen colour of golden-yellow.

Equivalent Ranks: (Note that from 1942 on, riflemen were named Grenadiere (line infantry); or Jaeger (light infantry).) In other arms, as in the British army, specialist terms were used as follows: artillery: Kanonier; Cavalry; Reiter; Engineers: Pionier, when referring to private soldiers.

German Army	Waffen SS	British	American
Generalfeldmarschall	Oberstgruppenführer	Field-Marshal	General (5-star)
Generaloberst	Obergruppenführer	General	General
General der . . . (1)	Gruppenführer	General	Lieutenant-General
Generalleutnant	Brigadeführer	Lt-General	Major General
Generalmajor	Oberführer	Major-General	Brigadier
Oberst	Standartenführer	Colonel	Colonel
Oberstleutnant	Obersturmbannführer	Lt-Colonel	Lt-Colonel
Major	Sturmbannführer	Major	Major
Hauptmann	Hauptsturmführer	Captain	Captain
Oberleutnant	Obersturmführer	Lieutenant	Lieutenant
Leutnant	Untersturmführer	2nd Lieutenant	2nd Lieutenant
Stabsfeldwebel	Untersturmführer	Staff Sergeant	Master Sergeant
Hauptfeldwebel	Sturmscharführer	RSM	First Sergeant
Oberfeldwebel	Hauptscharführer	Sergeant-major	Master Sergeant
Feldwebel	Oberscharführer	CSM	Technical Sergeant
Unterfeldwebel	Scharführer	Sergeant	Staff Sergeant
Unteroffizier	Untersharführer	Sergeant	Sergeant
Obergefreiter	Rottenführer	Corporal	Corporal
Gefreiter	Sturmmann	Lance Corporal	Acting Corporal
Oberschutze	Oberschutze	Private	PFC
Schutze	Schutze	Private	Private

NB: Some ranks are not exact equivalents; especially at field rank and above.

60. Waffen SS Officers' Uniforms. (HU 1066)

Table 8 TYPICAL INFANTRY WEAPONS

Piece	Calibre in (mm)	Weight in (kg)	Length in (cm)	Rate of Fire (rpm) Cyclic	Rate of Fire (rpm) Practical	Max Range (metres) Theoretical	Max Range (metres) Practical	Ammunition Feed	Remarks
Pistole 08 (Luger)	9·00					800 (with stock)		8-round mag.	
Pistole 38 (Walther)	9·00	2·00				200	100	8-round mag.	
MP 40	9·00	4·30	86·0	500	180	200	100	32-round mag.	Used Pistole 08 ammunition
MP 44	7·92	5·40	94·0	500	180	up to 800	—	35–38-round mag.	As for Karabiner 98k
Fallschirmgewehr 42	7·92	5·00	112·0*	660	—	1200	—	20-round mag.	As for Karabiner 98k
Karabiner 98k	7·92	3·90	111·0	—	5	up to 1200	—	5-round clip	
Gewehr 41	7·92	4·05	113·0	—	10	up to 1200	—	2×5 round clips	As for Karabiner 98k
MG 34 lmg	7·92	11·50	122·0	900	100–120	2000	6–800	Belt or drum (50-rd. belts)	As for Karabiner 98k
as-hmg	7·92	19·10†	122·0	900	300		2000	Belt or drum (50-rd. belts)	
MG 42 lmg	7·92	10·80	124·5	1200	250	As for MG34	As for MG34	As for MG 34	
as-hmg		19·00	124·5	1400	500				
5cm le Gr W 36	50·00	14·00	46·5	—	12–20	—	521·0	HE only	
8cm Gr W 34	81·0	56·70	114·3	—	12–20	—	2380·0	HE & Smoke	
12cm Gr W 42	120·0	282·00	785	—	6	—	5940·0	HE only	

7
Tactical Signs
and Symbols

Tactical signs and symbols used by the German army can be divided into three interrelating groups:

(i) basic unit/weapon/arm of service/transport symbols for order of battle charts and unit organisation charts

(ii) map signs and other indications for plotting friendly and enemy positions and similar information (eg minefields, barbed wire)

(iii) identification and warning signs in the field, especially on vehicles and signposts.

These signs and symbols did not remain constant throughout the war. On a large scale, as equipment, etc, became more complicated, so did the signs. For instance as gun calibres increased, this was shown by adding bars or strokes to the basic weapon sign until the original pattern was almost obscured. It was therefore decided in 1942 to revise parts of the scheme to clarify it and remove anomalies; the result for a year or more was somewhat confusing as both old and new symbols were used indiscriminately and in combination. On a small scale, field units often produced modifications of the 'standard' symbols by accident and thus many variations existed, especially on vehicles. The examples shown in this chapter are, unless otherwise indicated, the official definitive patterns and should be used when referring to the various Order of Battle charts displayed elsewhere in this book.

Basic Symbols

These were used to indicate units, weapons, arm of service and type of transport, and could be utilised singly or in combination. Unit symbols were based on the platoon or equivalent sub-unit and were often linked with indications of the arm of service; the main ones are shown in Figs. 31/2, old symbols being given in one or two important cases. Companies and equivalent units were shown by the basic sign with a thickened left or right hand edge (Fig. 33) and, if different sub-units were involved as in an HQ company, by one of two insertions within the basic symbol: these could be letters (eg St for *Stabs*, or staff; v for *Verpflegungs* or food supply) or a collection of platoon symbols, sometimes with numbers and calibres of platoon weapons indicated also. Note that in the latter case, as with all combinations of major symbols these should be read from right to left – eg a 'heavy' company of a battalion will appear to the left of the three rifle companies.

Battalion-sized units and above were normally indicated on Order of Battle charts by a combination of these symbols with the appropriate weapon signs

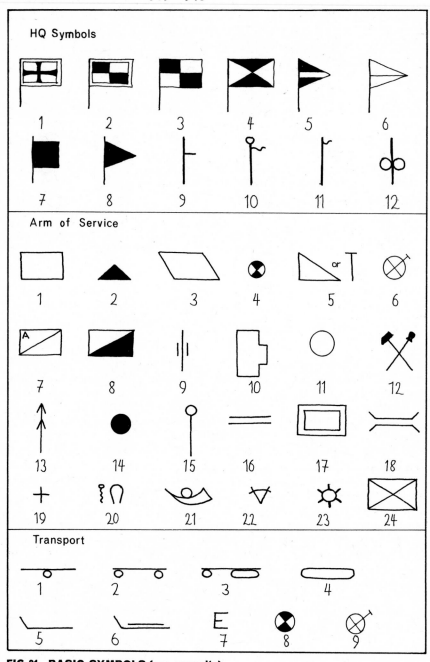

FIG 31 BASIC SYMBOLS (see opposite)

FIG 31. BASIC SYMBOLS

HQ Symbols:
(1) OKH; (2) Army Group (Heeresgruppe); (3) Army; (4) Corps; (5) Division; (6) Brigade; (7) Regiment; (8) Abteilung or equivalent; (9) Company; (10) Panzer unit; (11) Recce unit; (11) Motorised (partly motorised has one wheel bisected by flag-staff). 10–12 were used in combination with 1–9.

Arm of Service:
(1) Infantry; (2) Mountain Tps; (3) Panzer Tps; (4) Bicycle Tps; (5) Old and 'new' Anti-tank; (6) Motor-cycle Tps; (7) Recce Tps; (8) Cavalry (also pre-1943 recce); (9) Artillery; (10) Signals (11) AA (under weapon sign); (12) Construction Tps; (13) Engineer Tps; (14) Rly Operating Tps; (15) Transport (supply); (16) Supply (columns); (17) MT Park; (18) Bridging Tps; (19) Medical; (20) Veterinary; (21) Field Post Office; (22) Mapping and Observation; (23) MT servicing; (24) Unit Transport – sometimes used for Divn. Services in general, with added letters (eg Fp = Field post). These symbols could be used in combination.

Transport:
(1) Partly motorised; (2) Motorised; (3) Half track; (4) Fully Tracked; (5) Ski Tps; (6) Sledge; (7) Railway; (8) Bicycle; (9) Motor-cycle. These symbols indicate the nature of a unit not that all vehicles in it are of the type shown.

and 'type of transport' symbols shown in Fig. 32. Note that individual unit numbers within the organisation are shown above the basic symbol – as occasionally were artillery ranges where appropriate – weapon calibres or the notations 's' (heavy), m (medium), le (light) to the left of the appropriate weapon sign, and numbers of a weapon within a unit are to the right of or below its symbol. Where a composite number (eg 4 + 33) is shown, this normally indicates different types, the heavier weapon(s) being shown to the left; it was not normal to show personnel numbers or personal weapons on these charts. Armoured units in infantry formations were distinguished by the half-track symbol and the note 'gp' (gepanzerte) and in AFV units by an abbreviated vehicle description (eg III = Tank III) within the unit symbol, often combined with a cipher showing long or short barrel gun – l(ang) or k(urz). Other common additions were self-explanatory symbols such as an axe (butchery coy) or a symbolic loaf (bakery), while occasional word abbreviations appeared in obscure situations. The main ones were Nachr(ichten) – signals; Nachsch(ub) – supply or support; vers(tärkte) – strengthened; vers (orgungs) – maintenance; and the notes 'mot' – motorised; and 'mot Z' (motorised platoon within a unit).

Note too that foreign equipment was normally denoted by the addition, in brackets, of a small letter using the code below:
b – Belgian; d – Danish; e – English; f – French; h – Dutch (hollandsche); j – Jugoslav; n – Norwegian; ö – Austrian (Österreich); p – Polish; r – Russian; t – Czech (tscheco . . .).
HQ signs and symbols were basically flags, normally combined with the basic symbols but sometimes on their own. Practice seems to have been inconsistent although subordinate HQs within a Division often sported a version of their arm of service sign on the 'flagstaff'.

For large scale diagrams, a further set of symbols was in use as shown in

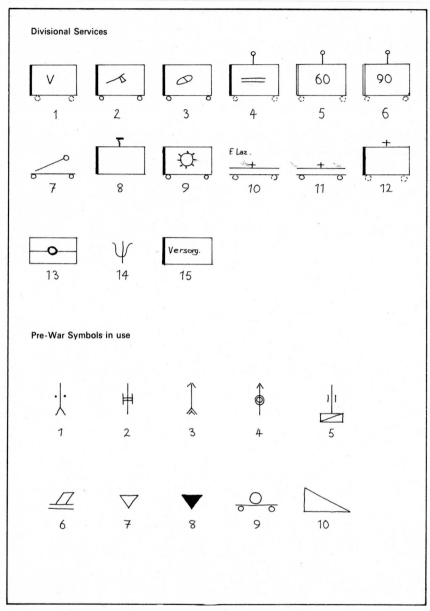

FIG 32 MISCELLANEOUS SYMBOLS (see opposite)

FIG. 32. MISCELLANEOUS SYMBOLS

Divisional Services:
(1) Verwaltungs (food and pay); (2) Butchery; (3) Bakery; (4) Supply handling company; (5) and (6) Typical transport companies incorporating several columns; (7) Field Police (Feldgendarmerie or Ordnungspolizei); (8) Veterinary Company, Repair Company (MT), Field Hospital; (11) Field Ambulance Company; (12) Medical Company; (13) Map reproduction office; (14) Band; (15) Maintenance and support.

Pre-War Symbols in Use:
These symbols in particular tended to linger on throughout the war: (1) Heavy machine gun; (2, 3 and 4) Methods of showing increased calibres in artillery pieces by means of bars, tails and circles; (5) Cavalry units; (6) Mortar; (7) Survey; (8) Photographic section; (9) Map reproduction section; (10) Anti-tank units.

Fig. 34, whereby details of personnel and their weapons could be given; these were usually matched with a list for easy cross reference.

Map Symbols

The symbols normally overprinted on tactical maps showed the units involved, with their positions so far as possible; and the presence and type of any known defence works.

(i) unit symbols were in general an adaptation of those described above and consisted of the basic unit symbol thickened throughout with additional data surrounding it; the most important item was the unit number but it could also include major weapons and ranges. Fig. 35 gives examples.

(ii) defence positions were mostly self-explanatory but examples of the more obscure ones are given in Fig. 35.

Identification and Warning Signs in the Field

IDENTIFICATION SIGNS

These, which appeared both on motorised vehicles and, with modifications, on flags, signboards and other plaques, were of two basic types:

COMBAT IDENTIFICATION SIGNS: These were officially restricted to front line vehicles and comprised variations on the national insignia, with large identification letters and numbers of various patterns. The nazi swastika was little used for this purpose except as part of the national flag which in the early years of the war was often draped over the top of vehicles to identify them to friendly aircraft.

Crosses (*kreuzen*), however, were widely used, mainly for ground identification of AFVs; as the photographs in this book show, patterns differed widely with local painting but in general German built, and therefore easily recognised, vehicles had small black-filled crosses on the sides and rear, while larger white-outline crosses adorned captured or unfamiliar vehicles.

In addition to the insignia, tactical numbers were provided to enable a unit commander easily to recognise and communicate with individual vehicles within his unit. These were normally three-figure numbers of which the first showed

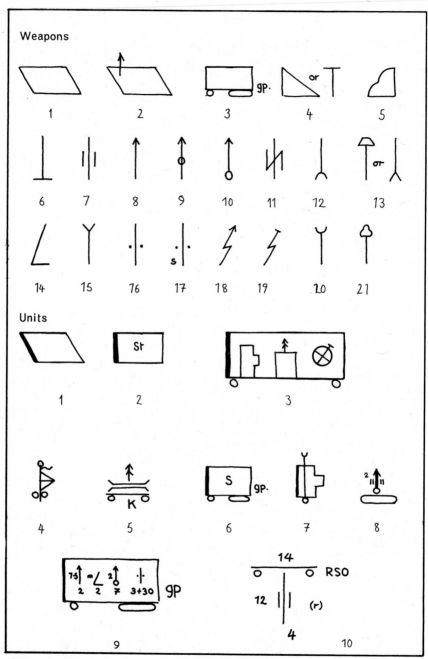

FIG 33 WEAPON AND UNIT SYMBOLS (see opposite)

FIG. 33. WEAPON & UNIT SYMBOLS

Weapons:
(1) Tank; (2) Assault gun; (3) Armoured infantry; (4) Anti-tank; (5) Armoured car;
(6) Infantry gun; (7) Gun-howitzer; (8) Gun (Kanon); (9) Howitzer; (10) AA gun;
(11) Recoilless gun; (12) Infantry anti-tank weapon; (13) 'Smoke' mortar; (14) Mortar; (15) Flamethrower; (16) Light machine gun; (17) Heavy machine gun; (18) WT;
(19) WT intercept; (20) Telephone coy; (21) Telephone constr.

Units:
(1) Tank company or battalion; (2) HQ Company (infantry); (3) HQ Coy (alternative
display pattern); (4) HQ of motorised Panzer Grenadier Brigade; (5) Engineer
bridging column with Brückengerät K; (6) Heavy company of an armoured infantry
unit; (7) Telephone Coy (partly motorised); (8) Company of quadruple 20m AA
guns on fully tracked chassis; (9) Detailed method of showing armoured infantry
rifle company; (10) Battery of four 12cm captured Russian gun-howitzers towed by
Raupenschlepper Ost. Max range 14km.

the company within the mother unit, the second the Zug or platoon within that
company, the third indicating the individual vehicle within the platoon. HQ
vehicles carried distinctive ciphers consisting of either a capital R (Regiment) or
a big Roman I, II or III (Abteilung) with a two-figure number from 01 to 09
indicating specific Officers (eg R01 was the regimental commander). Within
the companies certain combinations also identified the sub-unit commanders
and their aides: 01 the company commander, 02 the CSM, while platoon
leaders took 11, 21, etc. Thus the commander of 3rd Zug in the 2nd kompanie
of the 2nd Abteilung (6th company in the regiment) would be 631.

These numbers were officially restricted to tank units, armoured infantry
and armoured engineer units, armoured infantry companies of the recce
Abteilung and unit staff armoured vehicle up to Regiment level. They were
normally displayed prominently on armour or turret sides and rear in a variety
of types. Originally they were on detachable rhomboid boards, presumably to
facilitate transfer to a replacement vehicle, but these were replaced after the
French campaign by painted numbers usually a white outline with black or red
centre depending on the vehicle camouflage. In practice these codes were also
used by some SP artillery and assault guns which officially had battery letters
instead, and by some armoured units that should have come under the scheme
outlined below.

NON-AFV IDENTIFICATION SIGNS: These were normally unit or sub-unit
identification signs but in two distinct series – Divisional or organic abteilung
(eg assault gun brigade) signs; and tactical insignia for lesser units.

DIVISIONAL SIGNS

Every Division or Brigade had its own identifying symbol as in other armies.
Examples are given in Fig. 36 but in general the less potent the unit the more
elaborate was its sign. Thus the Panzer Divisions normally had strictly simple
signs in yellow or white; the few exceptions were those reformed from infantry
units fairly late on or were SS. These insignia were at times changed or swapped
between Divisions for security reasons and examples of variations are shown.

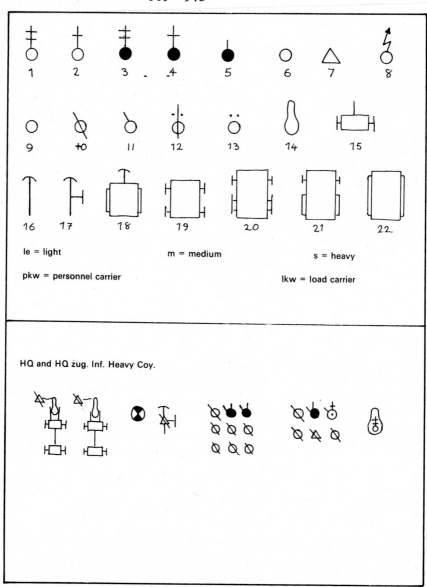

FIG 34 LARGE SCALE SYMBOLS

(1) Unit Commander; (2) Officer; (3) Senior NCO; (4) NCO; (5) Lance-corporal or equivalent; (6) Private; (7) Vehicle driver; (8) Radioman; (9) Pisto-armed; (10) Riflemen (or carbine); (11) machine pistol; (12) Machine gunner; (13) Ammunition carrier for MG; (14) Horse; (15) Horse-drawn vehicle – no of wheels indicated as for motor vehicles; (16) Motor bicycle; (17) Motor-cycle combination; (18) Motor-cycle tractor; (19) 4-wheeled MT; (20) 8-wheeled MT; (21) Half-track MT; (22) Fully-tracked MT.

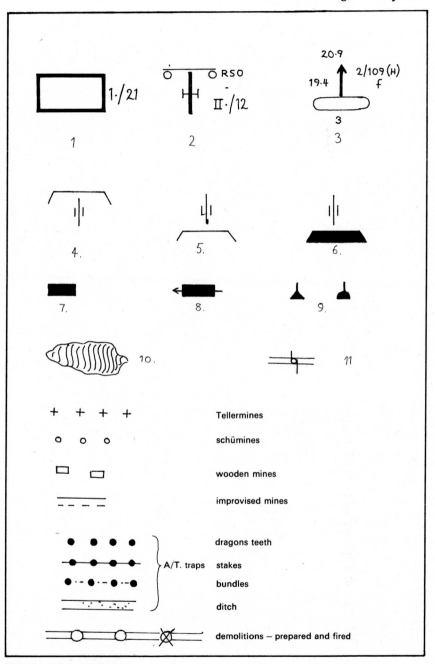

FIG 35   MAP SYMBOLS

(1) 1st Battalion of Infantry Regt. 21; (2) 2nd Batterie of Artillery Regt. 12 (or 2nd Abteilung); (3) Batterie of three heavy French guns from 2nd Abteilung of 109 Army artillery regt.; (4) Artillery in position; (5) Ditto in fixed position; (6) Ditto in fortified position under concrete; (7) Casemate; (8) Gun in casemate; (9) Artillery observation positions; (10) Zone of fire; (11) Road block.

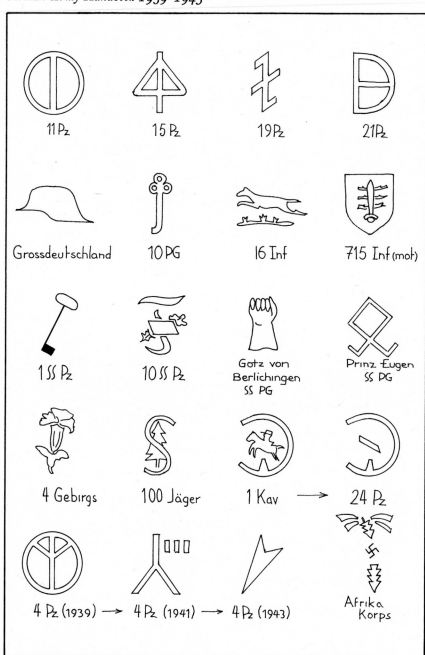

FIG 36 DIVISIONAL SIGNS

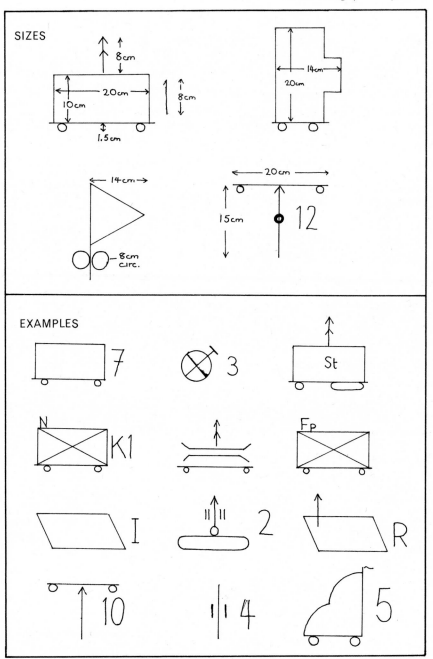

FIG 37 VEHICLE SYMBOLS

Infantry Divisions, on the other hand, usually had quite elaborate heraldic or pseudo-heraldic emblems based on their territorial associations and these were normally retained throughout a Division's career. The Divisional sign normally appeared on all vehicles and was extensively used on signposts, etc.

TACTICAL INSIGNIA

These were based on the symbols described earlier in this chapter but adapted for their particular purpose. They were officially applied to all motor, and many horse-drawn vehicles other than AFVs and there were standard sizes and positions for them (Fig. 37). The latter were the front left-hand mudguard or front armour plate, and the rear mud flap or tailboard. Those for motorcycles were half size and applied to front and rear mudguards. In practice, however, size and shape and position all varied, only the yellow or white colouring being standardised. These signs were also used on signboards and indicator posts to denote unit areas in a large camp or assembly area.

OTHER FIELD SIGNS: Other markings found were standard lettered signs, often in Gothic characters, indicating the direction and position of various HQs and administrative formations, and the various pieces of information often painted on vehicles – weight restrictions, etc. The most important of these were the vehicle numberplate, each consisting of two letters and six or seven numbers and carried by all motor transport. There were various series of which the most important were WH – army; WL – Luftwaffe; WM – Navy; and SS (as the formalised double-lightning flash) for the Waffen SS. The army also had such things as minefield warning signs and other items, often produced in differing forms to indicate 'true' and 'dummy' hazards to the initiated.

AIR-GROUND RECOGNITION SIGNS

These were either various combinations of light signals, fired from signal pistols, or else patterns made by laying out strips of cloth. The light signal varied widely.

Appendix 1

Summary of the Army's conduct of the War, with Important Dates (Figs 38–42)
1939

Following the annexation of Austria in March 1938, and the uncontested occupation in October of that year of the Sudetenland area of Czechoslovakia on the excuse that its population was largely German, Hitler declared Bohemia and Moravia, almost half of Czechoslovakia, a protectorate in March 1939. When this drew no overt action from the other Western powers he went further. On September 1st the Germans invaded Poland and, after a lightning campaign of only 18 days, occupied the country and parcelled it out with the Russians. This campaign, however, precipitated France and Britain into declaring war.

IMPORTANT DATES

March	15	Bohemia and Moravia become German Protectorate
Sept	1	Germany invades Poland
	3	France and Britain declare war

1940

The German army spent the winter of 1939–40 building up its strength and then pursued two very successful campaigns. In April, Denmark and Norway were subdued, in May and June another Panzer-led Blitzkrieg smashed through the Netherlands and Belgium, drove the British from France and forced the French to ask for an armistice; France was divided into an occupied and unoccupied zone, the latter having a puppet government. A projected invasion of Britain scheduled for mid-September had, however, to be called off when the Luftwaffe failed to achieve the necessary air superiority. On the other hand Finland, Hungary, Rumania and the rest of Czechoslovakia became actively allied to Germany and contributed Divisions to the German army.

IMPORTANT DATES

May	10	Offensive in the west opens (Plan Gelb)
	20	Panzers reach channel coast
June	4	Fall of Dunkirk
	22	Franco–German Armistice
	24–5	Battle of France ends
July	16	Orders issued for invasion of Britain (Seelöwe)
Oct	12	Seelöwe (Sealion) postponed indefinitely
Nov	20–24	Hungary, Rumania, Slovakia join Axis
·Dec	18	Führer Directive No 21 for the invasion of Russian (Barbarossa)

1941

This was a year of decision in that Hitler opened three new fronts and in so doing committed the German army beyond its resources.

(a) In February, a two-Division force soon to become the Afrika Korps

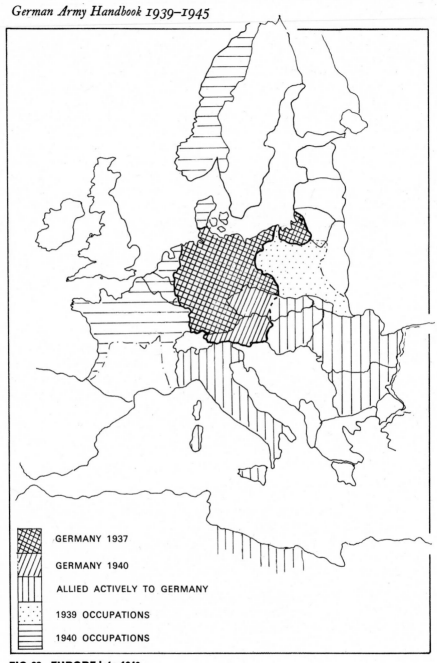

GERMANY 1937

GERMANY 1940

ALLIED ACTIVELY TO GERMANY

1939 OCCUPATIONS

1940 OCCUPATIONS

FIG 38 EUROPE late 1940

was despatched to North Africa under Lt-Gen Erwin Rommel allegedly to stiffen the Italian army there. It soon proved the mainstay of the African front and was able to contain the major British offensive during the year.

(b) In March and April a quick campaign brought control over Yugoslavia and Greece, belated British help being decisively repulsed and its survivors pushed back to the island of Crete. Crete in its turn was captured in ten days by the first and last major German airborne invasion – which virtually destroyed the German parachute force as an effective airborne arm. The British intervention did, however, seriously delay the third campaign:

(c) In this, the Germans committed themselves to a war on two major fronts by attacking Russia in June. In a Blitzkrieg campaign calculated to last only 8–10 weeks, they were defeated by the vast distances, by the resilience of the Russians, and by the late start caused by the Balkans campaign. Among severe disagreements between OKH and the field commanders as to where the main blow(s) should fall, the military effort became divided and the spearheads bogged down amid the mud of the Russian autumn without either capturing the vital capital of Moscow or completely defeating the Russian army. Caught unprepared for the severe Russian winter, the German army suffered a considerable setback. Hitler formally took command of OKH in December to impose his will on the army. Waffen SS fighting Divisions were committed for the first time during this campaign.

IMPORTANT DATES

Jan	11	Decision to establish a German presence in Africa. (*Sonnenblume*)
Feb	12	Rommel arrives in Africa, first troops following on 14th
March	27	Führer Directive No. 25 – to crush Yugoslavia
April	6	Balkans campaign opens
	17	Yugoslavia capitulates
	21–5	Greece capitulates
	30	End of resistance in Greece
May	20	Airborne invasion of Crete
June	1	British evacuation of Crete complete
	22	Russian campaign opens
Sept	19	Capture of Kiev
Oct	2	Beginning of Battle for Moscow (*Taifun*)
Dec	19	Hitler takes over direct command of OKH

1942

1942 was the high-water mark of the German war. In Russia the German army attacked once again and seized the Ukraine and the Crimea, but it failed to capture Leningrad and was finally halted at Stalingrad in November; there the Germany 6th Army, after trying and failing to take the city, was surrounded by the Russians. Elements of 22 Divisions were caught in the pocket.

In Africa, after startling successes that brought the Panzerarmee Afrika to the gates of Egypt, the German/Italian force was first halted and then forced on to the defensive at El Alamein; in November it had to retreat. Simultane-

FIG 39 LIMITS OF GERMAN EXPANSION

ously, early in November, allied landings commenced in French North Africa (Operation Torch). The Germans made their last major land acquisition by occupying the rest of France.

IMPORTANT DATES

Jan	21	Rommel counter attacks in Africa
Feb	8	Speer made Minister for Munitions, leading to rapid increases in production of war material
April	5	Führer Directive No 41 – summer offensive in Russia
May	17–25	Battle of Kharkov
	26	Start of Rommel's major offensive (*Theseus*)
June	28	Summer offensive in Russia opens
July	1	Fall of Sebastopol
Aug	18	Abortive raid in force by British and Canadians at Dieppe
Sept	3	High point of African campaign. Rommel halted before Alamein
	6	Germans invest Stalingrad
Oct	23	Battle of Alamein opens
Nov	5	German retreat in Africa begins
	8	Operation Torch starts
	11	Germans occupy rest of France (*Attila*)
Mid-Nov		Stalingrad encircled by Russians
Dec	12	German attempt to relieve Stalingrad opens

1943

The year of the first big German defeats. In Russia, after an unsuccessful relieving attempt, Stalingrad fell on February 2nd with a loss of some 91,000 men and much material. The Germans launched a winter offensive that achieved temporary gains around Kharkov but their major summer operation, '*Zitadelle*' (Citadel) to pinch out a big Russian salient near Kursk, failed and in so doing consumed the German mobile reserves. The Russians attacked on a long front and by the end of the year the German army had been pushed back west of Kiev.

In Africa, despite substantial reinforcements, the end came in May when Army Group Tunisia, which included Afrika Korps, surrendered – a total of over 250,000 men and much material. In July the allies invaded Sicily and took it after hard fighting. In September they invaded Italy whose Government surrendered five days later; the Germans took control and fought a long hard delaying action which by the end of the year had the allies still halted south of Rome at Monte Cassino. Increasing partisan activity in the Balkans kept a number of badly needed German divisions pinned down there.

IMPORTANT DATES

Jan	6	Russians raise seige of Leningrad
Feb	2	Stalingrad falls. German 6th Army lost
	21	German winter offensive in Russia around Kharkov
May	13	Army Group Tunisia surrenders

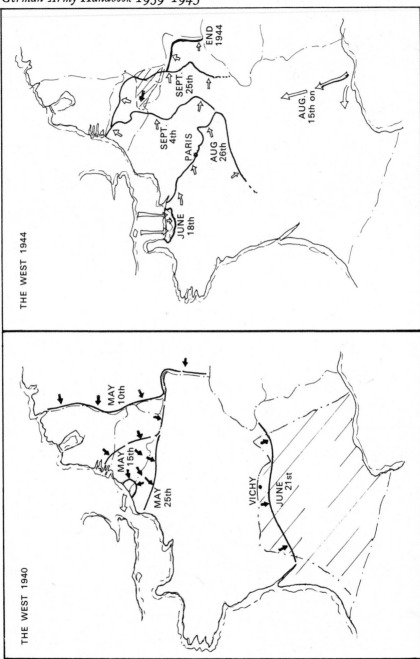

FIG 40   WAR IN THE WEST

July 5 Operation Zitadelle begins
 10 Allies invasion of Sicily
Sept 3 Allies invade Italy
 8 Italians surrender. German forces start take over
 9 Allied landing behind enemy line at Salerno. Beachhead contained by German forces
 10 Germans occupy Rome

1944

At the beginning of the year the Russians crossed the 1939 boundary of Poland and throughout the winter kept up continual pressure. In the south they cleared the Crimea and in the centre, partly owing to Hitler's refusal to allow retreat, they smashed Army Group Centre and encircled Minsk, taking over 100,000 prisoners. By the end of the year they were well into East Prussia, Slovakia and Hungary; Rumania was forced to surrender in August and Finland followed a few days later.

In Italy the allies advanced slowly in face of determined opposition and thorough resistance, their chance only coming after the Gustav Line at Monte Cassino was broken in May after months of hard fighting. Once on the move, however, the German army was pushed back to the Gothic Line between Rimini and Florence. Fortunately for the Germans, American insistence on a landing in the south of France – Operation Anvil, in August – proved a faulty decision. Hitler could afford to give up the area and it merely diverted Divisions from Italy, thus relieving the pressure; indeed the Germans were able to pull some of their strongest formations out to help on other fronts.

In the west, the long-heralded invasion of France took place in Normandy on June 6th. Helped by the German division of command which hampered local deployment of mobile reserves, the allies obtained a firm foothold and, after severe fighting, broke through at the end of July. Much of the German western armies were caught in the so-called Falaise Pocket in August, the rest pulled back before a swift campaign that brought American forces to the German frontier near Trier (Moselle) by September 17th. But resistance in Belgium and Holland was stronger. The airborne attempt to seize all bridges to the Rhine was only partially successful, the final one at Arnhem being retained by the Germans. The allied advance was temporarily halted at the 'Westwall' and December saw the last big German gamble – a winter offensive through the Ardennes for which, almost incredibly, they managed not only to collect 26 good Divisions but to assemble them without the allies finding out what was intended. The offensive was only narrowly defeated but it destroyed the last remaining German strategic reserve and so hastened the war's end.

IMPORTANT DATES

Jan 4 Russians cross 1939 Polish eastern border
 22–3 Allied landing behind German lines in Italy at Anzio Bridgehead contained by rapid German improvisation
March 4 Russian offensive in Ukraine opens
May 18 Allies break through at Monte Cassino; Anzio breakout

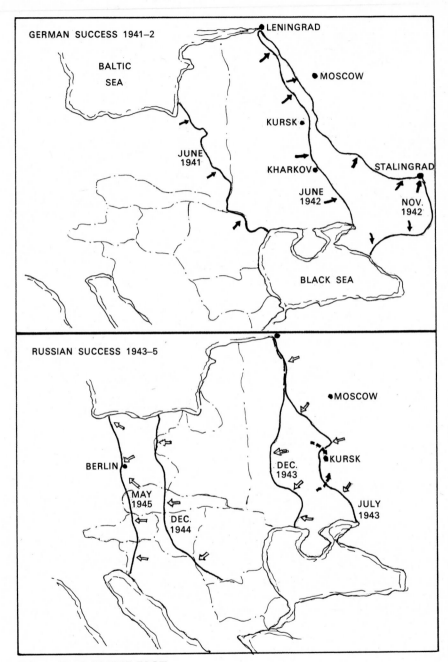

FIG 41 WAR IN THE EAST

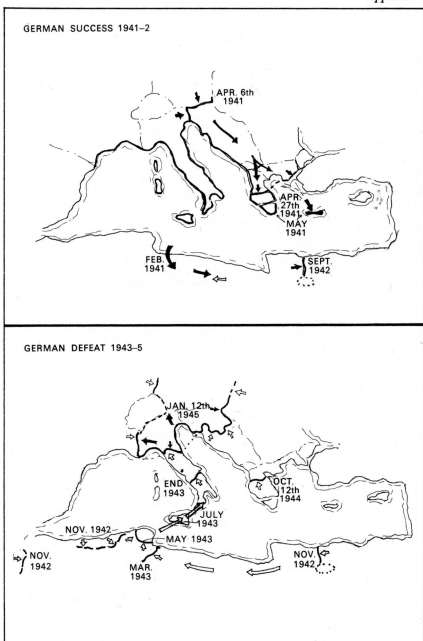

FIG 42 WAR IN THE SOUTH

June   4   Germans evacuate Rome
        6   Operation Overlord, invasion of France, opens
     22   Large scale Russian offensive against Army Group Centre
July   31   Allies break out from Normandy beachhead
Aug   4   Germans evacuate Florence
    4–6   Finland and Bulgaria surrender
    6–7   German major counter attack at Avranches (N. France) fails
    15   Operation Anvil, invasion of south of France, opens
 15–20   Closing of Falaise Pocket
    23   Rumania surrenders
    25   Liberation of Paris
Sept   11   US Army unit reaches German frontier
    25   Führer Directive to establish the Volksturm or Home Guard
Oct   3   Germans evacuate Athens
Nov   2   Greece liberated
Dec   16   German Ardennes offensive opens

1945

This year saw collapse on all fronts with the Russians determined to reach Berlin first – which they did. In April the Italian front collapsed and its commander surrendered. The army in the east and west nonetheless fought fiercely if unco-ordinatedly until the end in May. Hitler committed suicide.

IMPORTANT DATES
Jan   12   Russian winter offensive; E. Prussia reached by 23rd
    13   German retreat in the west begins
April 21   German front in Italy collapses. Surrender in Italy follows
May   7   Unconditional surrender of German forces in west. Cessation of hostilities follows

Appendix 2

Deutsches Afrika Korps (DAK)

The only real reason for singling out DAK for special mention among any other Corps of the German army is that, like the British 8th Army, it became a legend in its lifetime; its fame is even more unusual when one remembers that, while its famous opponent was the complete allied African army, DAK was officially only one corps among several in a largely Italian army which always greatly outnumbered it in size. The military importance is that it was the first German attempt to provide a modern force suitable for use in hot climates and it learned its lessons the hard way.

The Afrika Korps had its origins in Führer Directive No 22, issued on January 11, 1940, which recognised that the Italians were in serious trouble in

Africa and ordered the formation of a special 'blocking' force for dispatch to Tripoli.

Initially certain units from 3rd Panzer Division, including an HQ, were extracted to form the nucleus of a new 5th *Leichte Division* which, by February 1941, comprised the following units: a strong, partly armoured recce Abteilung; one panzer grenadier regiment of two partly armoured machine gun Abteilungen with engineer and infantry gun companies; two strong anti-tank battalions, and a two-Abteilung Panzer Regiment with 70 Pz II and 80 Pz III (5cm L/42) and Pz IV (7·5cm L/24), together with a 12-gun artillery Abteilung, an AA unit and Divisional services; an aircraft recce squadron was attached. This Division was transferred to Tripoli during Feb/March 1941 under the command of Lt-Gen Erwin Rommel and was very soon supplemented by 15 Panzer Division, at standard establishment. 5th Leichte Division was itself reconstituted as 21 Panzer Division at the beginning of August 1941.

These two powerful units always formed the nucleus of DAK but were supplemented between August and September 1941 by the so-called Afrika Division, a high quality motorised infantry formation built up especially for tropical service; this was later renamed 90th Leichte (Afrika) Division and became famous under that name.

These units, together with several 'independent' army units – heavy AA, artillery, etc, formed DAK as part of the Panzer Armee Afrika which was formally established as from January 22, 1942. The only significant reinforcements were another specially formed mobile infantry unit, 164th Leichte Afrika Division, which arrived in July and August 1942, and the Ramcke Parachute Brigade from 2nd Fallschirmjäger Division which came towards the end of that July. The Korps fought as separate units at El Alamein in November, stiffening the Italian formations, and then provided the effective rearguard for the long retreat across the desert, to Tripoli and the Tunisian Peninsula. There, DAK became part of the hastily reinforced Armee Gruppe Tunisia, and its units shared in the general German surrender at Tunis in May 1943. Although rebuilt later, the similarly named units which took part in the latter stages of the war had little connection but the names with their illustrious predecessors – which is not to say that they did not fight well.

To put DAK into perspective, it is salutary to realise that in 1942 it was only one of four corps:

DAK: 15Pz; 21 Pz; 90 Lt. Div.
10 (It) Corps: Bologna Div. Brescia Div.
20 (It) Corps: Ariete Div (armd); Trieste Div. (mot).
21 (It) Corps: Pavia, Trento, Sabratha Divs. + stiffening German units:
        esp. 33 Recce Abt. and 15th Lorried Infantry regiment.

Even in August 1942, besides an unknown number of obsolete Pz IIs, it had only 166 Pz III – 73 having the L/60 gun – and 37 Pz IV, 27 of which had the long 7·5cm L/43 gun. These were complemented by some 240 war-worn Italian M13s that were no match for the Allied guns.

Arguments will rage for years about the quality of leadership on both sides in Africa. Leaving this aside it may be pointed out that much of DAKs tribulations were due to its political masters. The early mistakes of organisation due to ignorance of conditions – unsuitable clothing, lack of diesel engined vehicles, desert equipment – were at least partly rectified later but the theatre was always regarded as a sideshow and kept short of equipment. If it had been given the scale of support that the allies wisely provided by the time of El Alamein, and which were later uselessly poured into Tunisia, it might have been a different story.

Appendix 3

The Waffen SS

The organisation later known as the SS started in effect during the early 1920s as a personal protection squad for Adolf Hitler; initially some 200 strong and known as the Stosstrupp Adolf Hitler it soon became the *Schutzstaffel* (protective squad) and, hence, the SS. It was officially formed in 1929 when Heinrich Himmler became the first 'Reichsführer SS', commanding a force still under 300 strong; by the time Hitler came to power it had grown to over 50,000, mostly in what was called the *Allegemeine*, or general, SS. It was regarded as the military arm of the Nazi party, being a voluntary organisation with very strict racial and ideological requirements in its recruits, and the 'combat' side developed in two distinct ways from about 1935 on. First there were the true combat troops (*SS Verfügungstruppen*) which formed the Führer's personal bodyguard – the *Leibstandarte Adolf Hitler* which grew from one to four infantry regiments between 1935 and 1938; this was an elite force always intended to serve under army command in time of war.

The other, and more sinister, branch was the *SS Totenkopfverbände* (SS Death's Head troops) used to guard concentration camps and to carry out political operations in occupied countries. Starting with five battalions (*Sturmbanne* in SS terminology) in 1935, it had grown to four regiments (*Standarten*) by the end of 1938 and took part in the 'occupations' of Czechoslovakia and Austria.

Totenkopf and Verfügungs troops also took an active part in the 1939 Polish campaign and Hitler was persuaded, somewhat reluctantly, to allow an expansion of SS combat strength. Some of the Totenkopfverbände were formed into the nucleus of SS Totenkopf Division as early as October 1939, and in April 1940 the armed branch was formally established as the Waffen SS. It started with the equivalent of three motorised infantry divisions and one horse-drawn one. The latter was the so-called SS Polizei Division formed from security troops; the former were Leibstandarte Adolf Hitler, officially a strengthened regiment but soon in near-divisional strength, the SS Verfügungs Division, and Totenkopf.

At this stage in the war the position of the Waffen SS was not entirely favourable. Hitler was not very encouraging and the Wehrmacht High Command did its best to discourage SS recruitment in favour of its own while allocating supplies only grudgingly. Indeed for the first time the SS had to compromise with its racial purity ideals and recruit from the 'Germanen' or Volkdeutsche, people of German descent living in occupied areas who did not come under the normal Wehrkreis catchment areas.

Nonetheless the Waffen SS grew steadily during 1940 and 1941, first by forming autonomous regiments and then by turning more Totenkopf troops into the Kampfgruppe Nord (later a mountain Division) and the SS Kavallerie Brigade. A new motorised Division, SS Germania, was authorised late in 1940 mainly from Volksdeutsche personnel and this became SS Wiking from 1941 on to avoid confusion with the SS regiment Germania which was one of its constituents. In the same way, SS Verfügungs Division, first renamed SS Deutschland, later in 1941 became SS Das Reich.

In 1941, too, the Totenkopfverbände were finally assimilated into the Waffen SS either as the nuclei of new units or as reinforcements for existing ones. Many of the Allegemeine SS were also drafted to make up losses and further the expansion; all SS troops at this period came directly under army command as had been originally envisaged.

The pressure on recruitment continued and increasing use was made of foreign Nazi sympathisers. These 'volunteers' were used to fill up the elite units and to form their own '*Freiwillinge*' (volunteer) units. These troops, mainly West Europeans, were apparently in general quite good, although they raised problems of their own: an OKH comment on the failure of SS Wiking in one operation notes wryly that it was not for lack of fighting spirit but 'because so many officers had been killed that there were no longer sufficient with command of the necessary languages,' It would seem, however, that all such Divisions needed stiffening with German SS, for attempts during 1941–2 to form national Legions in various countries were not very successful; this was partly because original promises were not kept but also because the officers and NCOs did not have the same commitment to Germany. All four Legions were disbanded in 1943, the best elements being combined to form the Freiwillinge Panzer Grenadier Division Nordland.

Hitler still restrained the build-up of the SS to some degree, partly because of varying reports on their effectiveness as fighting troops, but the efficiency of four major units was increased early in 1942 by the addition of a tank battalion to each – in January for Leibstandarte and Das Reich, in May for Totenkopf and Wiking. In November 1942 they were further built up to strong panzer grenadier Divisions and redesignated as such. Meanwhile in May 1942 an SS Army Corps was formed under General Paul Hausser to control them – the first step to reducing the army's hold on the Waffen SS – and in July the SS Kavallerie Brigade became SS Kavallerie Division Florian Geyer. The year closed with the formation of a second SS Corps controlling two new panzer grenadier Divisions, the 9th SS (Hohenstaufen) and the 10th SS (Frundsberg).

1943 was at once the high point and the beginning of decline for the Waffen SS. Although it had been given permission to recruit German volunteers, it attracted mainly the very young and fanatical (the average age in Frundsberg in 1943 was under 18). In consequence early in 1943 conscription was enforced, putting the SS again in direct competition with the regular Wehrmacht. Thus, although two new panzer grenadier Divisions were formed in the spring and summer, being 11th Freiwillinge and the notorious 12th SS Hitler Jugend, German replacements were not even sufficient to keep the existing units up to strength. Future drafts for the ever increasing number of units had to come more and more from racially 'impure' and often reluctant sources – Eastern European refugees, Balkan sympathisers, even Russian prisoners given the alternatives of fighting or forced labour.

As a result, although the personnel doubled between 1943 and 1945, while the number of Divisions officially reached 40 (38 numbered plus two Cossack Divisions), only three others, the largely Germanic 16, 17th and 18th panzer grenadier Divisions, had any pretensions to elite standard. The rest were poor quality infantry and were often Divisions in name only. Many never exceeded regimental strength and the proliferation which appeared during the last months of the war were often little more than figments of their creator's imagination. Of the impressed troops, only the three Divisions formed from citizens of former Baltic states showed much fighting spirit and that mainly, apparently, because they knew what would happen if they were overrun by the Russians.

On the other hand, the original elite Divisions were extremely fine troops and after their successes round Kharkov in March 1943 Hitler's attitude to them changed considerably. They were constantly strengthened and were well above the strength of supposedly superior army Divisions even before seven were officially designated full panzer Divisions in October 1943. These were Leibstandarte, Das Reich, Totenkopf, Wiking, Hohenstaufen, Frundsberg and Hitler Jugend; from that time on, they became Hitler's 'fire brigade' and received preferential treatment. Top-class fighting formations, constantly re-fitted in preference to other troops, they could be relied on to halt enemy attacks if it was humanly possible. Ironically, at the time, they were taken more and more out of local army control, to act as a strategic reserve under Hitler's direct orders – and such were these that at several crucial moments when they might have had a decisive effect on a battle they were not there. Nonetheless they retained their esprit de corps right up to the end and it is a minor legend that, at the final surrender when many of the remaining regular troops either just faded away or slouched wearily into captivity, the crack SS units first destroyed their equipment and then marched proudly in to surrender.

It is inevitable that in even a superficial tracing of Waffen SS history the question of atrocities arises. For some historians the SS should take the blame for all that happened; for SS apologists it was never the Waffen SS, always the political SS that committed the crimes, sometimes, like the notorious Dirle-wanger Brigade, dressed up as soldiers. The truth, as usual, lies somewhere between the two, though exactly where is never certain.

Undoubtedly much of the bad early reputation came from the original Totenkopfverbände which, though not of the army, were dressed in army-type uniforms and so unjustly passed on much blame. Undoubtedly, too, the Waffen SS troops did commit appalling atrocities. To name but two in the west, the Malmedy massacre in 1944 was perpetrated by a fighting unit, and the 1944 sacking of Oradour sur Glane by Das Reich has left a permanent scar over that part of France to this day – the village is still kept just as it was left after its buildings had been fired and its population butchered. Yet in justice to the whole force, these horrors were the work only of a minority and the bulk of the Waffen SS were simply hard fighting troops. There are plenty of instances before and after the second world war to show that if any nation trains men as professional killers to the standard required of an elite force, they will act as killers if provoked. Bestiality in war is an almost universal characteristic, not one possessed by the Nazis alone.

NB: Apart from their own particular terminology: Gruppe, Sturmbann, Standarte, for company, battalion, regiment, etc, the SS used regular army organisation, equipment and, with minor variations, uniform. The main variations are described at the appropriate points in the text.

Table 9   ROLL CALL OF SS DIVISIONS

Nr	Type (final)	Name	Remarks
1	SS Panzer Division	Leibstandarte Adolf Hitler	Formed from bodyguard troops
2	SS Panzer Division	Das Reich	Orig Verfügungs Division
3	SS Panzer Division	Totenkopf	
4	SS Panzer Grenadier	Polizei	
* 5	SS Panzer Division	Wiking	
6	SS Gebirgsdivision	Nord	From Totenkopf troops
** 7	SS Freiwillige Gebirgsdivision	Prinz Eugen	
8	SS Kavallerie Division	Florian Geyer	
9	SS Panzer Division	Hohenstaufen	
10	SS Panzer Division	Frundsberg	
*11	SS Freiwillige Panzer Grenadier Division	Nordland	Partly from National legions
12	SS Panzer Division	Hitler Jugend	Mainly from members of Nazi Youth Movement
*13	Waffen Gebirgsdivision der SS	Handschar	See footnote
*14	Waffen-Grenadier Division der SS	(Galiz nr 1)	
*15	Waffen-Grenadier Division der SS	(Lett nr 1)	
**16	SS Panzer Grenadier	Reichsführer SS	
**17	SS Panzer Grenadier	Götz von Berlichingen	
**18	SS Panzer Grenadier (freiwillige)	Horst Wessel	
*19	Waffen-Grenadier Division der SS	(Lett nr 2)	
*20	Waffen-Grenadier Division der SS	(Estn nr 2)	
†*21	Waffen Gebirgsdivision der SS	Skanderberg	Mainly Albanian troops
*22	Freiwillinge Kavallerie Division der SS	Maria Theresia	
†*23	Waffen-Grenadier Division der SS	Kama (Croat)	Designation used for PG Division Nederland, 1944
†24	Waffen Gebirgskarstjager Division der SS	—	Reputed of low quality Alpine troops
†*25	Waffen-Grenadier Division	Hunyadi	(Ungar nr 1)

Nr	Type (final)	Name	Remark
†*26	Waffen-Grenadier Division	(Ungar nr 2)	Both Hungarian origin
†*27	SS Freiwillige-Grenadier Division	Langemarck	
†*28	SS Freiwillige-Grenadier Division	Wallonien	
*29	SS Freiwillige-Grenadier Division	(russ nr 1)	Nr given to Italian SS in 1945
*30	SS Freiwillige-Grenadier Division	(russ nr 2)	
†*31	SS Freiwillige PG Division	Böhmen-Mähren	Established 1945 by school troops in Czechoslovakia
†32	SS Panzer Grenadier	30 Januar	Formed 1945 from training troops
†*33	Waffen Kavallerie Division der SS	(Ungar nr 3)	Annihilated 1945 and nr given to SS Charlemagne
†*34	SS Freiwillige Grenadier Division	Landstorm Nederland	
†35	SS Polizei Grenadier Division	—	Formed 1945
*36	Waffen-Grenadier Division	—	Dirlewanger Brigade upgraded
†*37	SS Freiwillige Kavallerie Division	Lützow	
†38	SS Panzer Grenadier	Nibelungen	Formed 1945 partly from staff of officers school at Bad Tolz

*Indicates partly or mainly from foreign troops.
**Indicates partly or mainly from Volksdeutsche.
†Indicates unit believed to have been only in regimental strength or below.

There were also several nominally battalion or regiment sized units including the two embryo Cossack Divisions and all made up of foreign troops except the crack Begleit Battalion (mot) Reichsführer SS and the Wachtbattalion (mot) Leibstandarte Adolf Hitler, which were bodyguard units.
Note: Divn Handschar: an odd unit which appears to have faded quickly but whose name was used as a cover for movement of other Divisions.

Bibliographical Notes

For those who wish to find out more about particular aspects of the German army there are two main ways:

(a) to buy some of the absolute flood of books and pamphlets of varying accuracy which have appeared in the last few years.

(b) to consult the basic source works from which most of these books – and indeed much of this book – have been compiled. These sources are mostly not easily available but can be consulted in specialist libraries such as that of the Imperial War Museum at Lambeth.

Source Books – General

1. *Kriegstagebuch des Oberkommandos der Wehrmacht* 1939–45
   6 vols Bernard & Graefe Verlag, Frankfurt, 1961.
2. *Das Deutsche Heer* 1939–45
   3 vols (unfinished) W. Keilig. Podzun Verlag, Bad Nauheim.
   This very detailed work is still in progress and consists of loose leaf pamphlets issued at intervals. So far, details of the main commanders and detailed orders of battle for all divisions have appeared.
3. *Das Heer, 1933–45*
   3 vols Mueller-Hillebrand.
   A useful general reference work on the army's background.
4. *British Notes on the German Army*
   War Office: various dates.
   These are intelligence reports issued to units in the field and provide comprehensive, if unillustrated, data on the enemy at a given period as seen from the opposing side. The 1940, 1941–2 and 1943 editions with subsequent amendments are available at the IWM and are very useful provided their shortcomings are realised.
5. *US Handbook on German Military Forces*
   US War Department 1945, reprinted commercially 1968 and available from Kirkgate bookstores, Leeds at £7. The reprint omits parts.
   A typically thorough American intelligence survey of the opposition as at the beginning of 1945, well illustrated and documented. A mine of information provided one remembers it is an Intelligence survey compiled during the war and contains the inevitable inaccuracies and omissions.
6. *Order of Battle of the German Army*
   Military Intelligence Divn, War Dept, Washington U.S.A. Various dates.
   This is exactly what it says.
7. *Feldgrau* 1951–2 *on*
   Periodical magazine published by Die Ordens Sammlung Verlag, Berlin. An excellent source of documentation on all aspects of the German army and its predecessors. It is the source of many later books and appears reliable – but when reading an article check later issues for readers corrections! A copy is held at the IWM.

Source Books – Equipment, etc.

8. *Illustrated Record of German Army Equipment* 1939–45
   5 vols. War office 1946. A very well documented and illustrated record of standard German equipment during the 2nd World War.
9. *Summary of German Tanks, 10/44*
   A contemporary SHAEF intelligence survey.
10. *Die Deutschen Panzer, 1933–45; Die Deutschen Geschütze 1933–45; Die Panzer Grenadiere.*
    All by General F. v Senger u Etterlin. J F Lehmanns Verlag, München. The basic source books on their subjects by an author very well qualified to write on the subject. An English edition of Die Deutschen Panzer,

updated and with additional information, has now appeared as German Tanks of WW2, a slightly misleading title since it covers all armour.

Some Other Sources of Information

11. Almarks series of monographs on various aspects of German arms in WW2. This is a series of booklets each dealing with a particular aspect of the German army: They vary in price from 6op to over £1·oo and the following titles are currently available:
    Wehrmacht Divisional Signs; German Combat Uniforms; Tactical Vehicle Signs; Waffen SS. Almarks Publishing Co., Edgeware. 1969 on.

12. *Military Vehicle Prints*
13. *Military Vehicle Data*

Two series of booklets, each booklet providing detailed data, drawings and photos of 3–4 Military vehicles.
Bellona Publications Ltd, Bracknell.

14. *Wehrmacht Illustrated* – a series of booklets offering very superficial 'historical data on a broad aspect of the German Army, but with a good selection of photographs. Currently available are:
    No 1 Afrika Korps; No 2 Panzerjaeger; No 3 Panzergrenadiere; No 4 Halbkettenfahrzeuge.
    All by Almarks Publications Ltd.

15. *German Tanks of WWII.* V Senger u Ettelin, translated by Ellis and Chamberlain. Arms & Armour Press. £4·80.

16. *German Infantry Weapons of World War II.* Lt-Col A J Barker. Arms & Armour Press. £1·25.

17. *History of the SS.* Stein.

18. *Die Panzer.* Stahl. Distr by Almarks.

19. *Die Fallschirmjaeger* 1936–45. Stahl 1970. Distr by Almarks. £2·25.

20. *Purnell's History of the Second World War.* Paperback series which includes volumes on specific aspects of the German army. 42½p.

21. *German Army uniforms and Insignia,* 1933–45. B. Davis, Arms and Armour Press, 1971 £4·25 – The definitive work on this subject.

This list is not exclusive! For those who read German the constantly increasing series of Divisional Histories is very valuable (the IWM has details of most) as is the wartime propaganda magazine Das Signal – the colour plates are superb. The IWM has some issues.

Index